Christmas is Coming!

**Compiled and Edited
by Linda Baltzell Wright**

Oxmoor House®

©1991 by Oxmoor House, Inc.
Book Division of Southern Progress Corporation
P.O. Box 2463, Birmingham, Alabama 35201

Library of Congress Catalog Card Number: 84-63030
ISBN: 0-8487-1043-6
ISSN: 0883-9077
Manufactured in the United States of America
Second Printing

Executive Editor: Nancy J. Fitzpatrick
Director of Manufacturing: Jerry Higdon
Art Director: Bob Nance
Copy Chief: Mary Jean Haddin

Christmas Is Coming! 1991

Editor: Linda Baltzell Wright
Assistant Editor: Alice London Cox
Illustrator and Designer: Barbara Ball
Editorial Assistant: Shannon Leigh Sexton
Assistant Copy Editor: Susan Smith Cheatham
Photographer: John O'Hagan
Photostylist: Connie Formby
Production Manager: Rick Litton
Associate Production Manager: Theresa L. Beste
Production Assistant: Pam Beasley Bullock

To find out how you can order *Cooking Light*
magazine, write to *Cooking Light*®, P.O. Box
C-549, Birmingham, AL 35283

Contents

Children's Workshop: Happy Holiday Crafts

Trimmings to Fix

Presents to Make

Parents' Workshop: Great Gifts for Children

Grin and Wear It

Just for Fun

Designers & Contributors

Dear Kids

What makes holidays special? Parties, of course! So this year the first chapter in *Christmas Is Coming! 1991* gives you a day-by-day plan for a holiday party that will be as much fun for you to give as it will be for your friends to attend. With a little help from a friend, you can make the invitations, decorations, favors, refreshments—even a party game.

After the party plans come ideas and instructions for "Presents to Make." You can frame your brother (at least a picture of him) and plant a windowsill herb garden for your mom. Design stationery for your dad and spray-paint a T-shirt for a friend. And when it's time to wrap all those presents, look in "Trimmings to Fix" for easy ideas like marbleizing paper with real marbles or turning a gift bag into an angel.

Before you begin any of the projects, though, check with a grown-up. Those projects labeled Level 1 are the easiest. Level 2 projects are simple, too, but take longer to complete, and the most difficult projects are labeled Level 3.

A Word to Parents

The miracle and memories of Christmas are never more apparent than in the faces of our own children. As a mother of two small ones, I don't know who gets more excited about the coming of the holiday— me or them. Through them, I find myself reliving Christmases past and encountering the pleasures of Christmas present. Their enthusiasm is so contagious!

You will see this same enthusiasm filling the pages of this book. For we know that children are the spirit of the season and the reason for *Christmas is Coming!*

Buddy Bear & Me

On the 1st day of Christmas
Buddy Bear helped me make
Plans for a Christmas Party

You will need (for each invitation):
A grown-up
Colored paper
Scissors
Colored markers
Wiggle eyes
Glue
Circle stickers or clear tape

1. Decide how many invitations you will need. Then **ask the grown-up** to photocopy the pattern on the next page onto the colored paper.

2. Cut out the invitation.

3. Use the markers to fill in the party information and address. Don't forget to color the designs.

4. Fold the invitation in half, with the star at the top as shown. Fold the invitation again, bringing the address side forward.

5. Unfold the invitation. Find the dot on the top of the letter R in the word "PARTY." From that point make a diagonal fold to the dot on the right of the star. Find the dot on the left of the star and make another diagonal fold. When you close the card, crease the fold in the star so that the point of the star folds down inside the card.

6. Color the eyes or glue wiggle eyes onto the star.

7. Fold the invitation so that the address is on the outside. Fasten the invitation with a circle sticker or tape it closed to the right of the address.

Come to a CHRISTMAS PARTY!

Time:
Date:
Place:

Given By

On the 2nd day of Christmas Buddy Bear helped me make
2 Ho-Ho Hats
and plans for a Christmas party.

You will need (for each hat):
Purchased party hat
Trims: colored pom-poms, hard candy, ribbon, colored paper
Glue
Scissors

1. Glue pom-poms or hard candy all around the hat. Let the glue dry.

2. To top the hat, make a bow from the ribbon and glue it on or cut a star from the colored paper and glue it on.

On the 3rd day of Christmas Buddy Bear helped me make 3 Flying Angels

2 ho-ho

You will need (for each angel):
1 roll of crepe paper
Scissors
Tracing paper
Pencil
10″ x 14″ piece of white drawing paper
Tape
Hole punch
4″ x 6″ piece of red-and-green plaid
  wrapping paper
Glue stick
Fine-point black marker
8″ piece of metallic star garland

1. Before you begin, decide where you want to hang your garland. Cut a strip of crepe paper to fit this space. Then decide how many angels you will need to hang on your garland.

2. Trace the patterns and cut them out.

3. Fold the white paper in half to make a 10″ x 7″ rectangle. Crease the paper along the fold. To keep the paper from shifting while you are working, tape the paper to a desk or table with the fold at the top.

4. Place the angel pattern on the paper. Line up the top edge of the wing (broken

line) with the folded edge of the paper and trace around the angel. Remove the pattern and cut out the shape through both layers. Use the hole punch to make an eye, punching through both layers.

5. Trace the patterns for the scarf, paw pads, and inner ear onto the wrapping paper. Cut them out and glue them to the front of 1 angel. With the marker, draw a mouth and nose.

6. For the halo, make a circle with the star garland. Twist the ends together. Unfold the angel and tape the halo to the back of the decorated angel's head. Then slip the angel over the crepe paper strip.

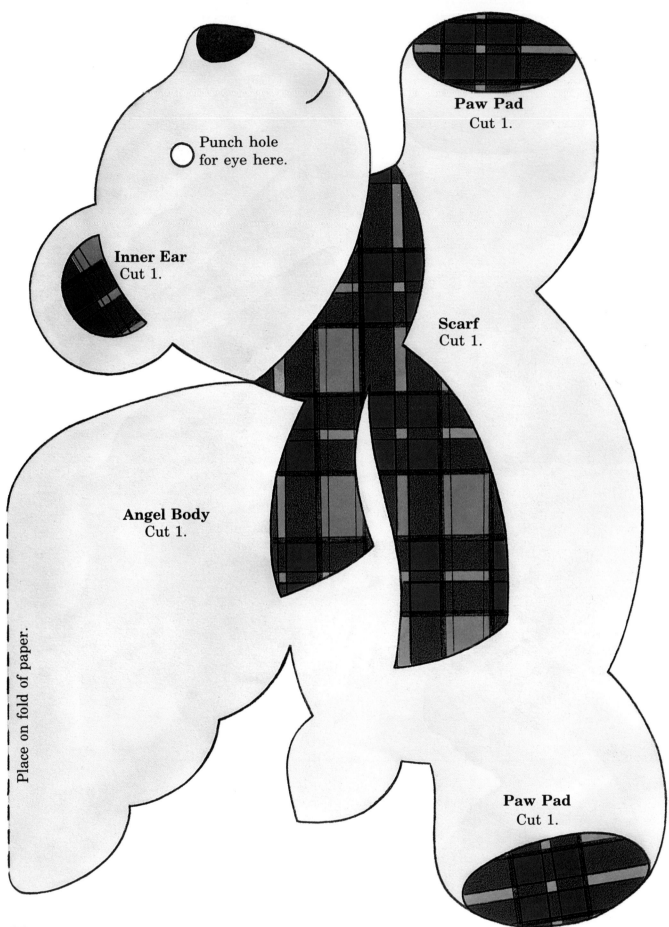

Punch hole for eye here.

Inner Ear
Cut 1.

Paw Pad
Cut 1.

Scarf
Cut 1.

Angel Body
Cut 1.

Place on fold of paper.

Paw Pad
Cut 1.

14

On the 4th day of Christmas Buddy Bear helped me make
4 Dancing Shoes

3 flying angels, 2 ho-ho hats, and plans for a Christmas party.

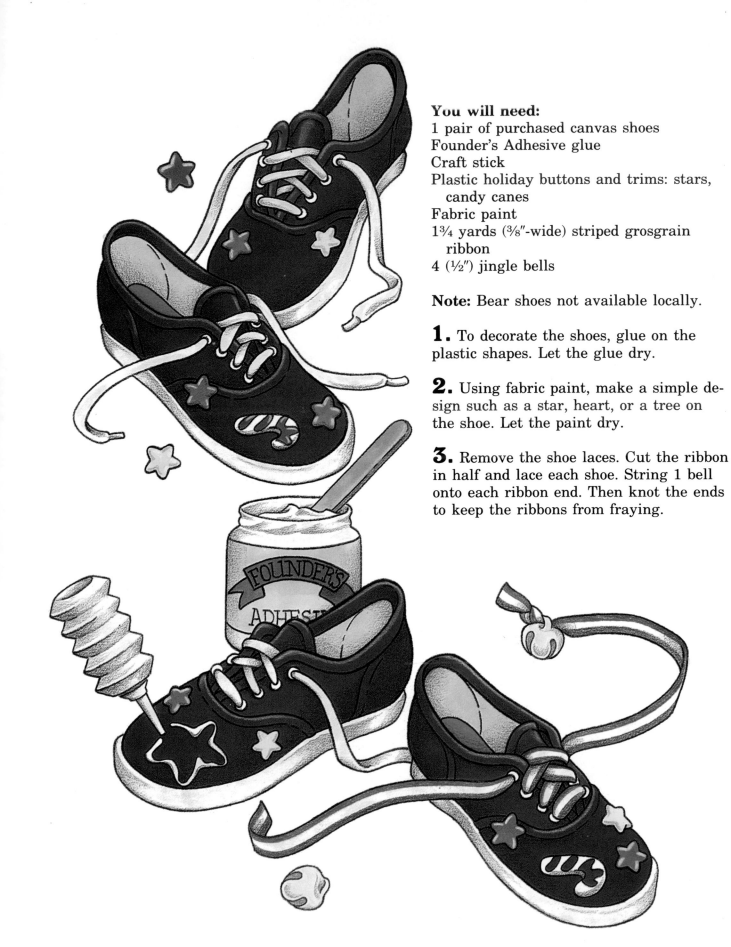

You will need:
1 pair of purchased canvas shoes
Founder's Adhesive glue
Craft stick
Plastic holiday buttons and trims: stars, candy canes
Fabric paint
1¾ yards (⅜"-wide) striped grosgrain ribbon
4 (½") jingle bells

Note: Bear shoes not available locally.

1. To decorate the shoes, glue on the plastic shapes. Let the glue dry.

2. Using fabric paint, make a simple design such as a star, heart, or a tree on the shoe. Let the paint dry.

3. Remove the shoe laces. Cut the ribbon in half and lace each shoe. String 1 bell onto each ribbon end. Then knot the ends to keep the ribbons from fraying.

On the 5th day of Christmas Buddy Bear helped me make
5 Golden Stars

4 dancing shoes, 3 flying angels, 2 ho-ho hats, and plans for a Christmas party.

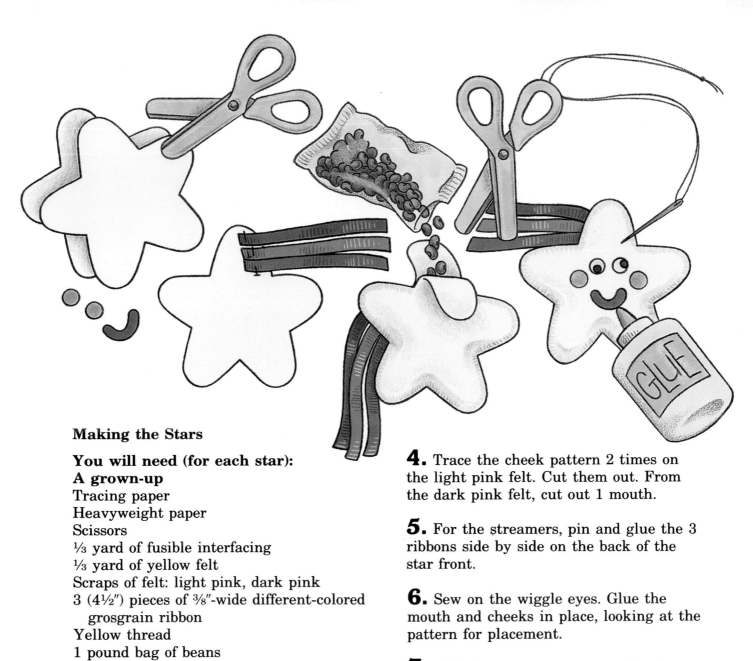

Making the Stars

You will need (for each star):
A grown-up
Tracing paper
Heavyweight paper
Scissors
⅓ yard of fusible interfacing
⅓ yard of yellow felt
Scraps of felt: light pink, dark pink
3 (4½″) pieces of ⅜″-wide different-colored
  grosgrain ribbon
Yellow thread
1 pound bag of beans
Liquid ravel preventer
Fabric glue
1 pair (⅝″-wide) sew-on blue wiggle eyes
Needle

1. Trace and transfer the patterns and markings to heavyweight paper and cut them out.

2. Ask the grown-up to apply the fusible interfacing to 1 side of the yellow felt for stiffening.

3. Trace the star pattern 2 times on the yellow felt. Cut them out.

4. Trace the cheek pattern 2 times on the light pink felt. Cut them out. From the dark pink felt, cut out 1 mouth.

5. For the streamers, pin and glue the 3 ribbons side by side on the back of the star front.

6. Sew on the wiggle eyes. Glue the mouth and cheeks in place, looking at the pattern for placement.

7. Ask the grown-up to sew the star together for you. With wrong sides facing and edges aligned, place the star front and back together. Zigzag-stitch along the outside edges, leaving 1 arm open. Fill the star loosely with beans. Zigzag the arm closed. Trim close to stitching.

8. Cut the ends of the streamers at an angle and coat them with liquid ravel preventer.

9. Make as many stars as you like. Then take turns tossing the stars through the holes in the tree into the box.

18

Making the Tree

You will need:
A grown-up
Craft paper
40″ x 60″ piece of foam-core board
Craft knife
Acrylic spray paints: green, red, yellow,
  pink, blue, orange
Glue
12″ square cardboard box
Masking tape
Scissors
Crepe paper strips: yellow, blue, pink,
  orange

1. **Ask the grown-up** to help enlarge
the pattern for the tree. Transfer all the
markings. Trace the pattern on the foam-
core board and cut it out, using the craft
knife. Cut 5 (7½″) circles in the tree (see
pattern). Then cut out shapes for decorations from the remaining foam core.

2. Paint the tree front green and tree
trunk red. Paint the tree decorations as
you like. Let them dry and glue in place.

3. Line up the lower edges of the cardboard box and the tree. Then tape the box
to the tree back. The box will help the
tree stand up and catch the stars.

4. Cut the crepe paper into 11″ streamers. Tape 8 streamers behind each hole.

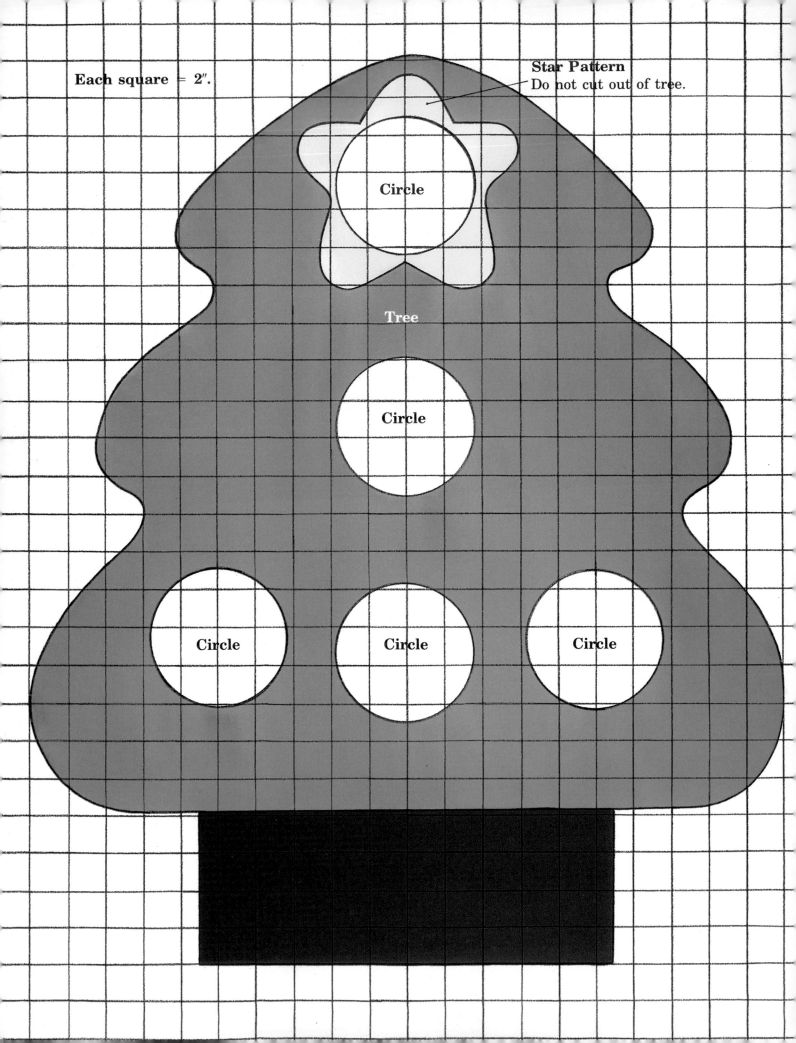

Each square = 2".

Star Pattern
Do not cut out of tree.

Circle

Tree

Circle

Circle

Circle

Circle

Ribbon
placement

Star
Cut 2.

Cutting line

Cheeks
Cut 2.

Mouth
Cut 1.

21

On the 6th day of Christmas
Buddy Bear helped me
make
6 Kazoos for Playing

5 golden

You will need (for each kazoo):
Glue
4½″ x 6″ piece of corrugated paper
Toilet paper tube
1 pound coffee can
Wax paper
Pencil
Scissors
Rubber band
Curling ribbon

1. Glue the corrugated paper around the toilet paper tube.

2. Stand the coffee can on the wax paper and trace around it. Cut out the circle.

3. Place the wax paper circle over 1 end of the kazoo. Hold the paper in place with the rubber band.

4. To decorate, tie a piece of ribbon around the rubber band and curl the ends.

5. To play the kazoo, place the open end over your mouth and hum a tune.

On the 7th day of Christmas Buddy Bear helped me make
7 Stockings for Stuffing

6 kazoos

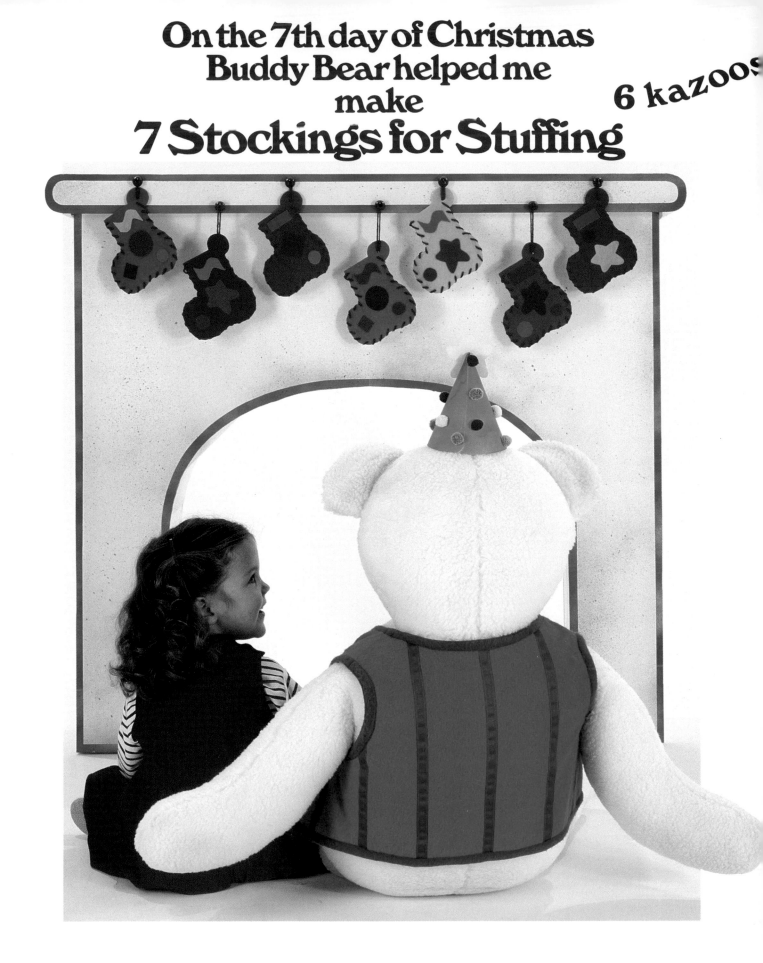

You will need (for each stocking):
Tracing paper
Sharp pencil
Scissors
¼ yard of felt
Scraps of colored felt
Hole punch
40″ of yarn
Large-eyed needle
Glue

1. Trace and transfer the patterns and markings. Cut them out.

2. From the felt, cut out 2 stockings. Be sure to mark the holes for stitching. Cut decorations from the scraps.

3. With the hole punch, make the hole for the hanger in the circle at the top of the stocking. Punch out the rest of the holes with the point of the pencil.

4. Thread the needle with the yarn. Knot 1 end of the yarn. Place 1 stocking on top of the other and hold them together. Start sewing on the side opposite the hanger circle. Sew through the holes all around the edges of the stocking. Then slide the needle off the yarn and make a loop through the large hole for the hanger. Tie the end of the yarn to the last stitch on the back of the stocking. Clip the end.

5. To decorate the stocking, glue the different-colored shapes to the stocking front.

Stocking
Cut 2.

26

On the 8th day of Christmas
Buddy Bear helped me,
make
8 Poppers Popping

7 stockings for stuffing, 6 kazoos for playing, 5 golden stars, 4 dancing shoes, 3 flying angels, 2 ho-ho hats, and plans for a Christmas party.

You will need (for each popper):
A grown-up
Scissors
1 toilet paper tube
Colored tissue paper
Wrapping paper
Ruler
Pencil
Glue stick
Small toy, candy, and a greeting written
   on a strip of paper
String

1. Ask the grown-up to cut the toilet paper tube in half. Cut 2 (6″ x 10″) rectangles from tissue paper. Cut 1 (6½″ x 9″) rectangle from wrapping paper.

2. Put the 2 halves of the toilet paper tube back together and treat them as 1 unit. Stack the 2 pieces of tissue paper. Center the tube unit on 1 long edge of the paper. Then roll it in the paper. The paper will extend beyond the ends of the tube. When you come to the edge of the paper, glue it in place.

3. Center the tissue-paper-covered tube unit on 1 long edge of the wrapping paper. The ends of the tissue paper will extend beyond the wrapping paper. Roll the tissue-covered tube in the wrapping paper. Then glue the long edge in place, leaving the ends open.

4. Insert a small toy, some candy, and a greeting into the tube through 1 end.

5. Wrap string 2 or 3 times around 1 end of the tube. Pull the string as tight as you can without tearing the paper. Then remove the string and fringe the ends of the papers with the scissors. Do the same thing to the other end.

6. To make your popper pop, hold 1 end in each hand and break it in half.

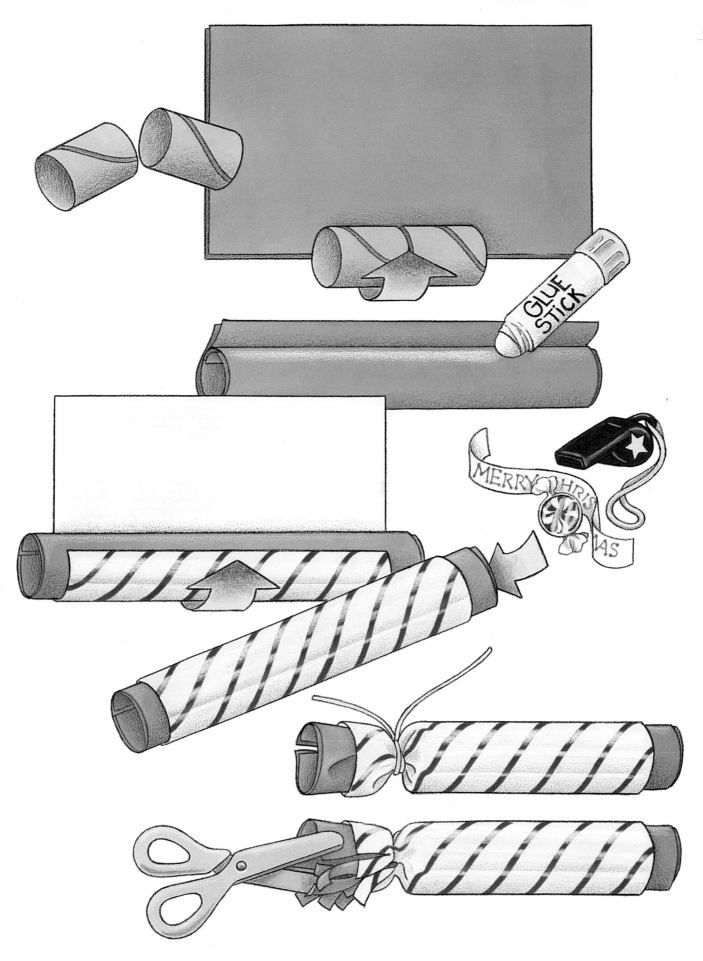

On the 9th day of Christmas Buddy Bear helped me make
9 Santas Sitting

a Christmas party.

You will need (for each bag):
Tracing paper and pencil
Scissors
White posterboard
Black flocked paper
Heavyweight red paper
Scrap of wrapping paper
Red bag (10″ x 5″)
Double-sided tape
Glue

1. Trace, transfer, and cut out patterns.

2. From posterboard, cut 4 cuffs (2 for the arms and 2 for the legs), 1 beard, 1 mustache, 1 hatband, 1 pom-pom, and 2 eyes. From black paper, cut 2 boot tops and 2 boot bottoms, 2 mittens, and 2 pupils. Cut 2 arms and 2 legs from red paper. Cut 1 bow tie from wrapping paper.

3. If you want Santa to hold a treat, put it in the bag. Then fold down the top corners of the bag and tape them in place.

4. To assemble the legs, glue the end of 1 leg to the top edge of the wrong (unflocked) side of the boot bottom where marked. Then line up the curved edges of the boot pieces and glue the boot top to the boot bottom and leg. Glue the cuff on where the leg and boot join. Fold up the boot at the edge of the boot bottom. Repeat for the other leg and boot.

5. To make the arms, glue 1 mitten, right side up, to the end of 1 arm. Glue on the cuff where the arm and mitten join. Repeat for the other arm.

6. To make Santa's face, place the bottom of his beard 1¼″ from the bottom of the bag and glue in place. Glue the hatband across the bag, covering the top edge of the beard. Glue the pupils to the eyes. Then glue the eyes in place. Glue the mustache just above the beard. Glue the bow tie at the bottom of the beard. Glue the pom-pom at the top of the hat.

7. Glue the arms between the folds in the sides of the bag.

8. Glue the legs on the bottom of the bag.

Hat Pom-pom
Cut 1.

Hatband
Cut 1.

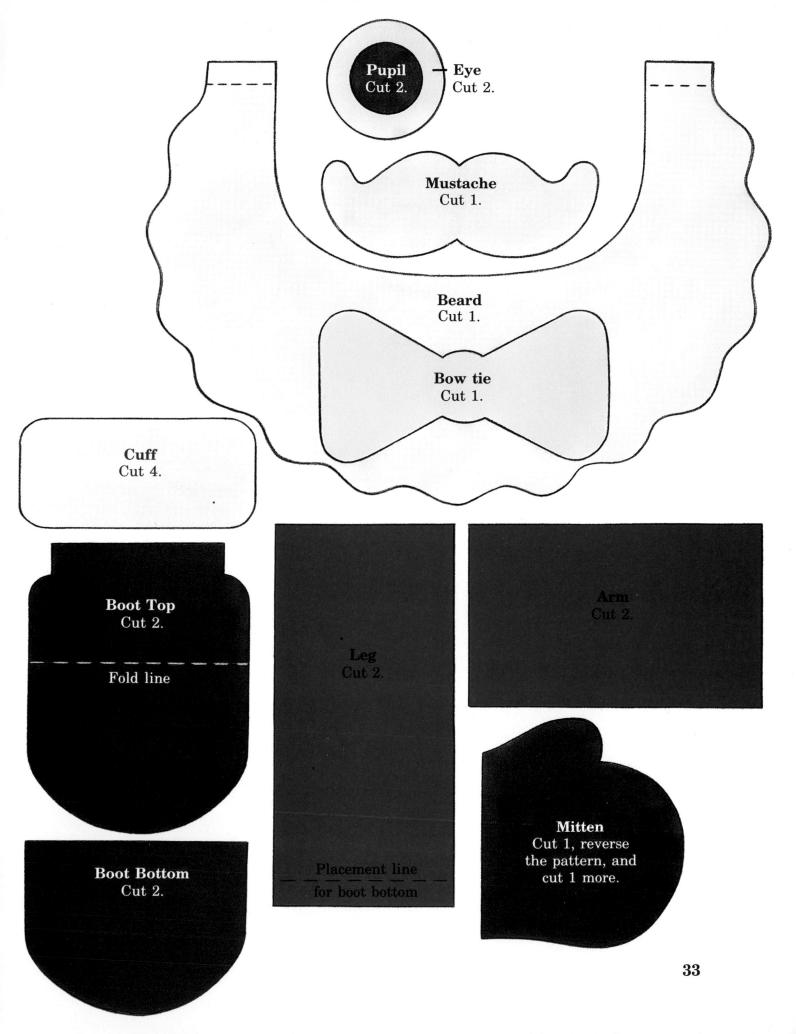

Pupil
Cut 2.

Eye
Cut 2.

Mustache
Cut 1.

Beard
Cut 1.

Bow tie
Cut 1.

Cuff
Cut 4.

Boot Top
Cut 2.

Fold line

Boot Bottom
Cut 2.

Leg
Cut 2.

Placement line
for boot bottom

Arm
Cut 2.

Mitten
Cut 1, reverse
the pattern, and
cut 1 more.

33

On the 10th day of Christmas
Buddy Bear helped me
make
10 Treats for Tasting

9 Santas

34

hats, and plans for a Christmas party.

sitting, 8 poppers popping, 7 stockings for stuffing, 6 kazoos for playing, 5 golden stars, 4 dancing shoes, 3 flying angels, 2 ho-ho

Royal Icing

You will need:
A grown-up
6 large egg whites
1 teaspoon of cream of tartar
Large mixing bowl
Electric mixer
2 (16-ounce) packages of powdered
    sugar, sifted

1. Ask the grown-up to help you combine egg whites and cream of tartar in the large mixing bowl. Beat at medium speed of the mixer until soft peaks form. Add half of the powdered sugar, mixing well. Add remaining sugar and beat at high speed 5 to 7 minutes. This will make about 4 cups of icing.

Note: This icing dries very quickly, so keep it covered with a damp cloth whenever you're not using it. Icing can be stored overnight, at room temperature, in an airtight container.

Bubblegum Boxes

You will need (for 10 boxes):
Royal Icing (recipe above)
3 tablespoons of water
60 (2½″) graham cracker squares
Plastic wrap
Paper towel
6 (2.1-ounce) containers of bubble gum
    tape
Plastic knife and wooden spoon

1. Measure out 1½ cups of royal icing and combine it with the 3 tablespoons of water to thin it. Stir until well blended. Keep the remaining icing covered.

2. Set 10 graham crackers aside. To paint the remaining graham crackers, crumple a piece of plastic wrap into a loose ball. Dip it into the thinned icing and tap it on a paper towel to remove any extra icing. Pat 1 side of a graham cracker with the ball to produce a "sponge-painted" look. Paint 49 more graham crackers the same way. Let them dry.

3. To make a box with the graham crackers, use the remaining icing as the glue. Spread a little icing along 2 opposite edges on the unpainted side of 1 cracker. Add the icing to the edges of 3 more crackers. Then carefully press the 4 graham crackers together to form a box. Let the box dry. Repeat to make 9 more boxes. You will use the 10 remaining painted crackers for the box tops.

4. For the bottom of the box, spread icing along all 4 edges of 1 unpainted graham cracker. Carefully set 1 box on top of this cracker. If necessary, add more icing. Repeat for the other 9 boxes.

5. To decorate the boxes, cut 140 (2½″) strips and 10 (1″) strips of bubble gum tape. Spread icing down the length of 4 (2½″) strips. Gently press 1 strip down the center of each side of 1 box. Repeat for the other boxes.

6. To decorate the box tops, spread icing down the length of 2 (2½″) strips. Press the strips onto 1 of the remaining painted crackers in a cross shape. Repeat for the other boxes.

7. To make the bows for the box tops, moisten the ends of 1 (2½″) gum strip with water. Make a loop with the strip and seal the ends by pressing them together. Make 3 more loops this way. Place the 4 loops together so that the ends are touching in the center. Press the center with the end of a wooden spoon until the strips are sealed together. Make

4 more loops and attach them to the center of the first 4, using the icing as your glue. Make a roll with 1 (1″) strip and glue it to the center of the bow with icing. Make bows for the other box tops.

8. Cut the remaining bubble gum tape into 20 (3″) strips. Notch 1 end of each strip to resemble the end of a ribbon.

9. With icing, glue 2 notched ribbon strips to 1 box top. Then add more icing and glue the bow in place. Carefully place the top on the box. Glue the remaining notched ribbon strips and bows to the other tops. Let them dry for 24 hours.

10. Fill your box with small candies and give as a party favor. Your guests can eat the candy and the box!

On the 11th day of Christmas Buddy Bear helped me make
11 Shakes for Sipping

10 treats

3 flying angels, 2 ho-ho hats, and plans for a Christmas party.

You will need (for 11 shakes):
A grown-up
10 (.6 ounce) chocolate peanut butter cups
2 quarts of vanilla ice cream
2 cups of milk
1 cup of powdered chocolate malted milk
1 (12-ounce) jar of chocolate fudge ice
    cream topping
Electric blender

1. Break each peanut butter cup in half.
Set them aside.

2. Ask the grown-up to combine 1
quart of vanilla ice cream, 1 cup of milk,
½ cup of powdered chocolate malted milk,
and half of the ice cream topping in the
container of the electric blender. Cover
and process the mixture 3 seconds. Then
remove the cover and take out the small
center piece. Replace the cover on the
blender.

**3. Ask the grown-up to watch as you
do this step.** With the blender running,
add 10 peanut butter cup halves, 1 at a
time, through the small opening in the
cover. Process the mixture just until it's
well blended. Pour it into cups and serve
it immediately.

4. Repeat these steps with the remaining ingredients.

On the 12th day of Christmas Buddy Bear helped me make

12 Friends Smile at Our Very Merry Christmas Party!

shakes for sipping, 10 treats for tasting, 9 Santas sitting, 8 poppers popping, 7 stockings for stuffing, 6 kazoos for playing, 5 g

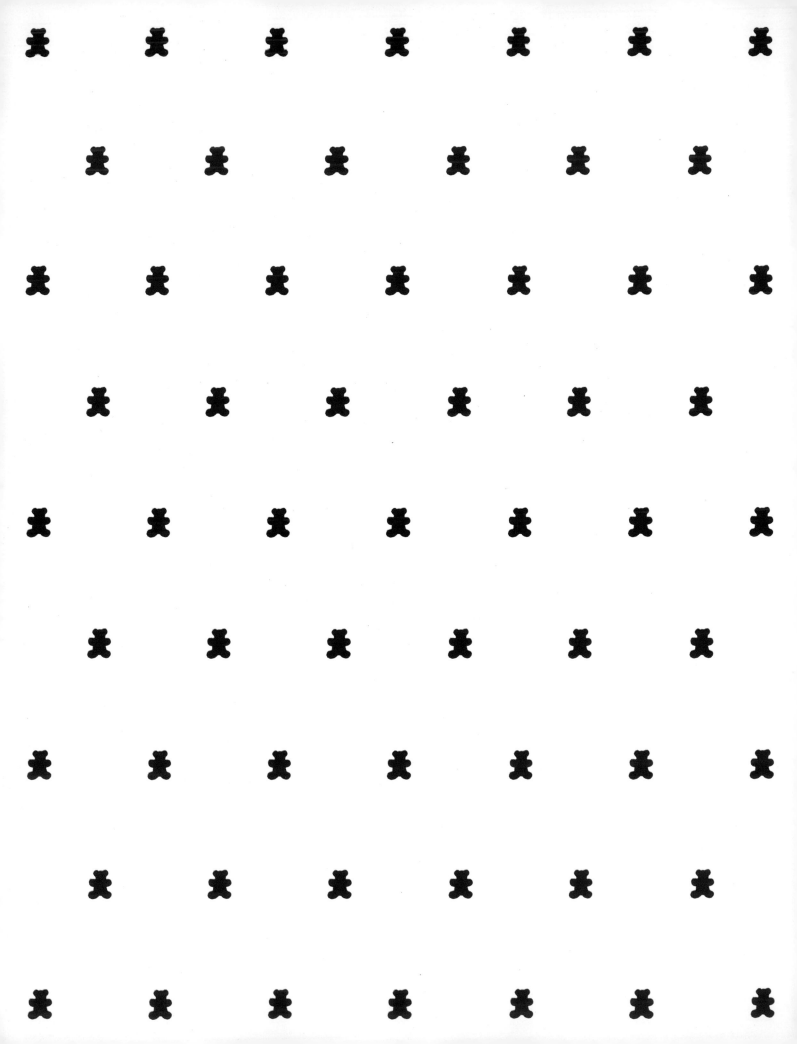

Children's Workshop
Happy Holiday Crafts

Angel Gift Bags

Pop a gift inside a colorful bag and add a cherubic face. Your angelic design will gather heavenly praises from family and friends.

You will need (for 1 bag):
Colored lunch bag
1 (6″) round paper doily
Stapler
3½″-diameter can
Pencil
Construction paper: pink, black
Scissors
Hole punch
Glue
Felt-tipped marker
2 small heart stickers
Multi-colored curling paper ribbon

1. Put a gift in the lunch bag. Fold the top edge closed.

2. Fold the doily in half and staple it over the top of the folded bag.

3. To make the angel's face, place the can on the pink construction paper and trace around it. Cut out the paper circle.

4. To make the eyes, punch 2 holes from the black construction paper. Glue them in place on the face.

5. With the marker, draw a smile. Place a heart sticker at each end of the smile.

6. To make the hair, curl 8″ strips of the ribbon with the blade of the scissors and glue the curls around the face.

7. Glue the face to the doily on the front of the bag, as shown in the photograph.

Marbleized Paper

It will be hard to decide which is more fun: painting with marbles or giving Christmas presents wrapped in one-of-a-kind wrapping paper. Be ready for ooh's and ahh's when you deliver gifts this holiday!

You will need:
A friend
Smocks
Newspaper
1 large sheet of white butcher paper
6 marbles
2 small paper cups
Acrylic paints: red, green
2 spoons

1. Put on a smock to protect your clothes from paint. If the weather is nice, this would be a good project to do outside. If you work inside, cover the floor where you are going to work with newspaper.

2. Place the butcher paper on the top of the newspaper.

3. Place half the marbles in each cup. Pour enough red paint in 1 cup to cover the marbles. Pour green in the other cup.

4. Using the 2 spoons, place the paint-covered marbles on the paper at different places.

5. Sit on 1 side of the paper and have the friend sit across from you on the opposite side. Take turns tilting the sides and corners of the paper to make the marbles roll to the opposite side. Gently move the paper up and down, letting the marbles roll around. Try not to let the marbles roll off the paper.

6. Put the marbles back in the cups for more paint and continue marbling until you are happy with your design.

7. Place books or other heavy objects on the edges of the painted paper to hold it down until it dries.

Level 1

Felt Faces

A few clips with your scissors and some dots of glue will turn plain frames and felt into fancy-faced Christmas ornaments.

You will need:
Plastic frames: 2 (2½″) round, 1 heart-shaped
Felt: pink, white, red, blue, orange, black
Pencil
Scissors
Glue
Hole punch
Small heart stickers: blue, green
Gold icicles
Silver tinsel pipe cleaner
Monofilament
6″ (½″-wide) ribbon

Angel

1. To make the angel's face, place the round frame on the pink felt and trace around it twice. Cut out the 2 circles.

2. Cut a mouth from the red felt and glue it in place on 1 pink circle. Hole-punch 2 circles from the blue felt and glue them at each end of the mouth. Add 2 blue heart stickers for the eyes.

3. Open the frame, remove the clear plastic insert, and place the face inside. Snap on the back of the frame.

4. To make the hair, curl 12″ lengths of gold icicles with the scissors. Glue them around the top of the frame.

5. For the halo, make a 3″ loop in the middle of the pipe cleaner and twist the ends together. Glue the ends of the halo to the middle back of the frame.

6. To finish the ornament, glue the other pink felt circle to the back of the frame.

7. To hang the ornament, cut a 10″ piece of monofilament and loop it through the hanger on the frame. Tie the 2 ends together.

Snowman

1. To make the snowman's face, place the round frame on the white felt and trace around it twice. Cut out the circles.

2. Cut a mouth from the red felt and glue it in place on 1 white circle. Hole-punch 2 circles from the pink felt and glue 1 at each end of the mouth. Add 2 blue heart stickers for the eyes. For the carrot nose, cut a triangle from orange felt. Glue it in place.

3. Trace and cut out the hat pattern. Trace the hat onto the black felt. Cut it out. Cut a strip of red felt for the hatband. Glue the band to the hat.

4. Open the frame, remove the clear plastic insert, and place the face inside. Snap on the back of the frame.

5. Place the hat just above the snowman's eyes and glue it to the frame. Tie a bow with the ribbon and glue it to the frame below the snowman's mouth.

6. To finish the ornament, glue the other white felt circle to the back of the frame.

7. To hang the snowman, cut a 10″ piece of monofilament and loop it through the hanger on the frame. Tie the 2 ends together.

Snowman's Hat

Santa

1. To make Santa's face, place the heart frame on the pink felt and trace around it twice. Cut out the 2 hearts.

2. To make Santa's hat, place the heart frame on the red felt and trace around just the lower half of the heart. Cut it out. Glue the red half heart to 1 of the pink hearts.

3. Cut a strip of white felt for the hat-band. Glue the band over the straight edge of the hat.

4. Stick 2 green heart stickers on the face for eyes.

5. Open the frame and remove the clear plastic insert. Place the face inside. Snap on the back of the frame.

6. Trace and cut out the beard pattern. Trace it onto the white felt. Cut it out. Glue the beard to the curved part of the frame, covering the hanger.

7. Hole-punch a nose from red felt. Glue it to the center of the beard.

8. Cut the pom-pom from the white felt. Glue it to the top of the frame.

9. To hang the ornament, cut a 10″ piece of monofilament. Fold it in half to make a loop and glue the ends to the back of the frame.

10. To finish the ornament, glue the other pink felt heart to the back of the frame.

Santa's Beard

Snowflakes

You won't see these giant snowflakes falling from a winter sky! But with scissors and tissue paper, you can cut some out to make a colorful blizzard and let it fall inside your house.

**You will need
(for each snowflake):**
A grown-up
Colored tissue paper
Scissors
Pencil
Tracing paper
Iron
Wax paper
Needle
Monofilament

1. Cut the colored tissue paper into a 10½″ square.

2. Fold the tissue paper square in half. Fold it in half again. Now, fold it in half diagonally to make a triangle. Then fold edge A to edge B. This will make a small triangle stick out on 1 end. Cut off that small triangle and set it aside.

3. Trace the pattern and cut it out. Then place the pattern carefully on the large folded tissue-paper triangle and trace the pattern. Keep the paper folded and cut along the solid pattern lines.

4. Ask the grown-up to help unfold the tissue paper snowflake and press it flat with a warm iron. Cut out 2 (11″) squares from the wax paper. Place the snowflake between the 2 pieces of wax paper and press it with the iron. The wax on the paper will melt and seal the snowflake inside. Trim the wax paper in a circle just outside the outer points of the snowflake.

5. To make a hanger for the snowflake, punch 2 holes in the wax paper circle with the needle. Cut a piece of monofilament as long as you need to hang your snowflake. Thread the monofilament through both holes and knot the ends.

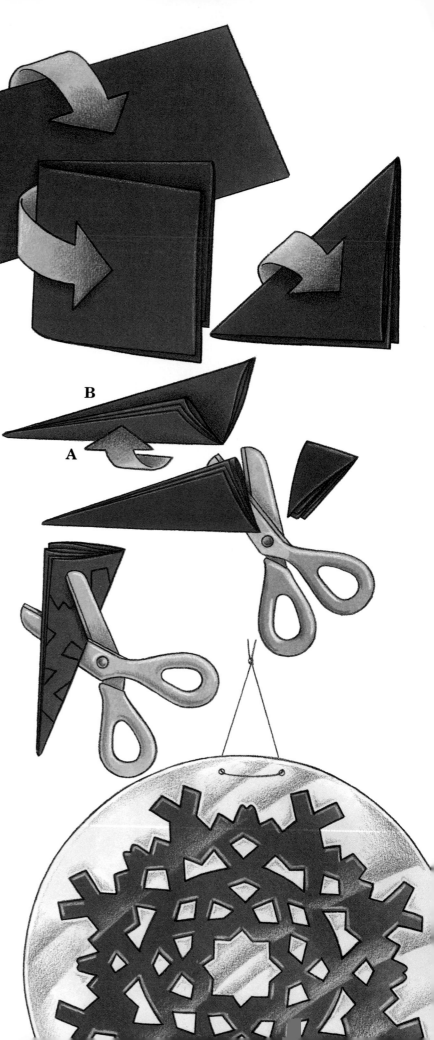

54

Glitter Tree

Light up your table this holiday with a glittery green-and-red decoration. And when the holidays are over, you can easily take it apart and save it for next Christmas.

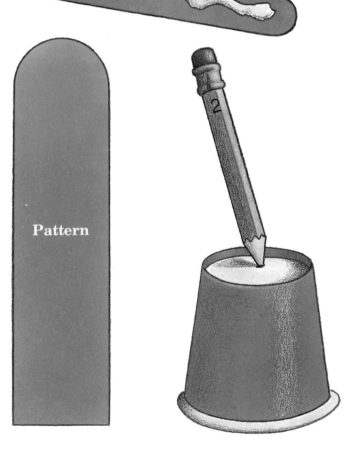

You will need:
Tracing paper
Pencil
Scissors
18″ x 24″ sheet of heavyweight green
   paper
Ruler
Hole punch
Glue stick
Red glitter
Green paper cup
Styrofoam
16″ (¼″-diameter) wooden dowel
Small amount of florists' clay
22 (16-mm) red wooden beads with ¼″
   holes

1. Trace and cut out the pattern.

2. Cut the green paper into 1″-wide strips. You will need 4 of each of the following lengths: 12″, 11″, 10″, 9″, 8″, 7″, 6″, 5″, 4″, 3″, and 2″.

3. To round the ends of all of the strips, place the pattern on top of each end and trace around it. Cut out the rounded ends.

4. Use the ruler to mark the center of each strip. With the hole punch, punch a hole at each center mark.

5. To decorate 1 side of each strip, draw a design with the glue stick; then sprinkle on the red glitter. Let the strips dry.

Pattern

6. To make the base for the tree, turn the paper cup upside down and make a hole in the center of the bottom, using a sharp-pointed pencil. Cut a block of Styrofoam to fill the cup. Push the dowel through the hole in the bottom of the cup and through the Styrofoam block. Slip the block into the cup. Then push the end of the dowel into a piece of florists' clay. (This will help hold the tree in place.)

7. Slip 2 beads on the dowel, sliding them from the top down to the cup. Slip 4 (12″) paper strips over the dowel and slide them down to the beads. Fan out the strips to make an 8-pointed star as shown.

8. Slip 2 more beads on the dowel. Then add the 11″ strips. Fan them out into the star shape. Continue placing beads and strips on the dowel, using shorter strips each time, until all of the strips have been used. Place only 1 bead between the 3″ and 2″ strips. Place the last bead on top of the 2″ strips to cover the end of the dowel.

57

Foldout Cards

A herd of reindeer, a band of angels, and a party of animals will be glad to carry your holiday hello to friends this Christmas season.

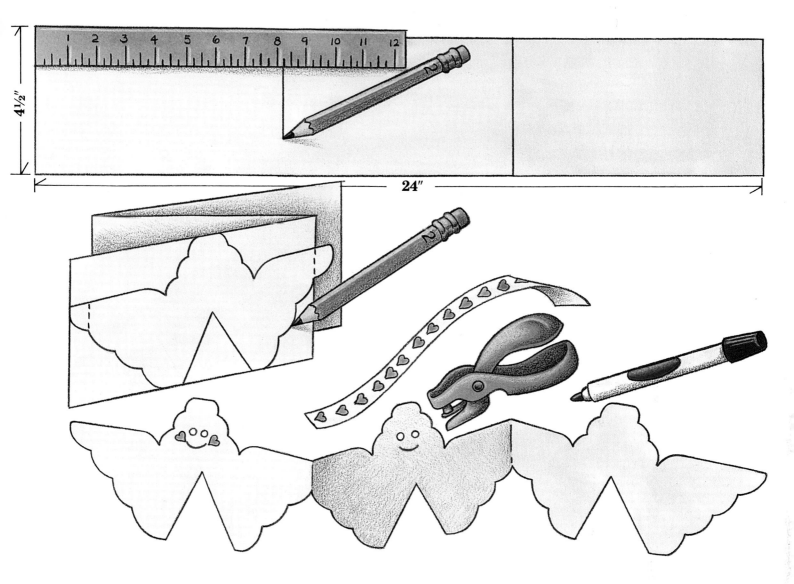

You will need (for 3 cards):
18″ x 24″ sheet of white heavyweight paper
Ruler
Pencil
Scissors
Tracing paper
Hole punch
3 (6″ x 9″) envelopes

For angel and reindeer:
Heart stickers
Red fine-point marker

Angel Card

1. From the white paper, cut a 4½″ x 24″ strip. Measure in 8¼″ from each end and draw a straight line. Fold the paper on these lines accordion-style (fold 1 forward, 1 backward). Set the paper aside.

2. Trace and cut out the angel pattern. Be sure to mark the broken lines. Center the pattern on the folded paper, with the broken lines of the wing tips lined up with the folds of the paper. The top of the head and the bottom of the wings will touch the top and bottom edges of the paper. Draw around the pattern and cut it out along the solid lines, through all 3 layers. (Do not cut on the broken lines.)

3. Unfold the card. Use the hole punch to punch out eyes. Stick 2 heart stickers on each face for cheeks, and use the red marker to draw a smile.

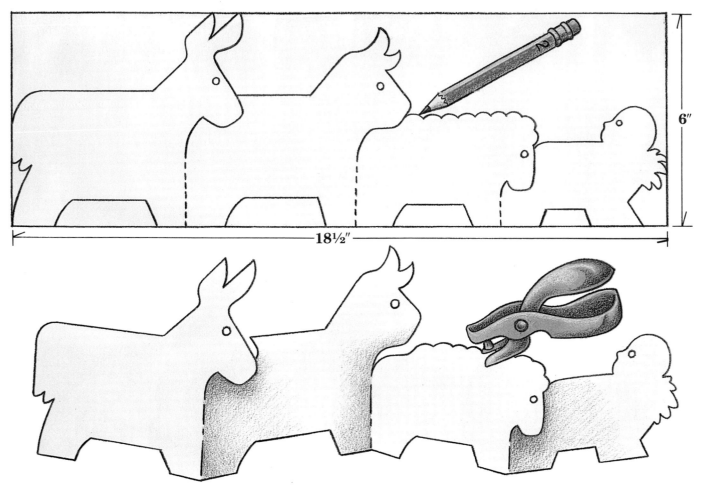

Nativity Card

1. Trace and cut out the patterns for the donkey, cow, sheep, and baby in the manger. Be sure to mark the broken lines. From the white paper, cut a 6″ x 18½″ strip. Line up the donkey's tail along the left end of the paper. Trace around the donkey pattern. Line up the back of the cow with the front of the donkey, with the broken lines touching. Trace around the cow pattern. Line up the back of the lamb with the front of the cow and trace around the pattern. Line up the foot of the manger with the front of the lamb and trace around the pattern.

2. Cut out the card on the solid lines only. (Do not cut on the broken lines.) Use the hole punch to punch out eyes. Fold the paper along the broken lines, accordion-style (like the angel), folding the line between the donkey and cow toward yourself.

Reindeer Card

1. Trace and cut out the pattern. Be sure to mark the broken lines. From the white paper, cut a 6¾″ x 16½″ strip. Line up the back legs on the pattern with the left end of the paper. Trace around the pattern. Then trace 4 more reindeer across the paper, lining up 1 reindeer's back legs with the front legs of the reindeer before him.

2. Cut out the reindeer on the solid lines only. (Do not cut on the broken lines.) Fold the card accordion-style (like the angel) on the broken lines.

3. Unfold the card. Use the hole punch to punch out eyes. Add heart stickers to the noses.

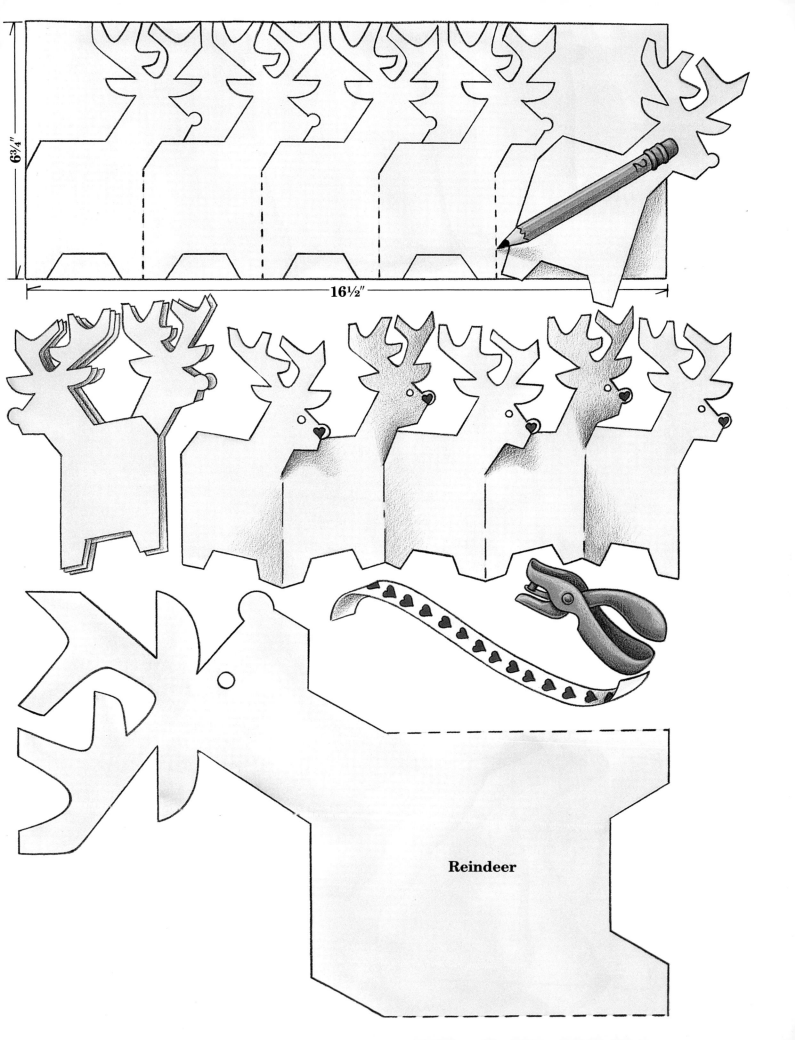

$6^3/_4$"

$16^1/_2$"

Reindeer

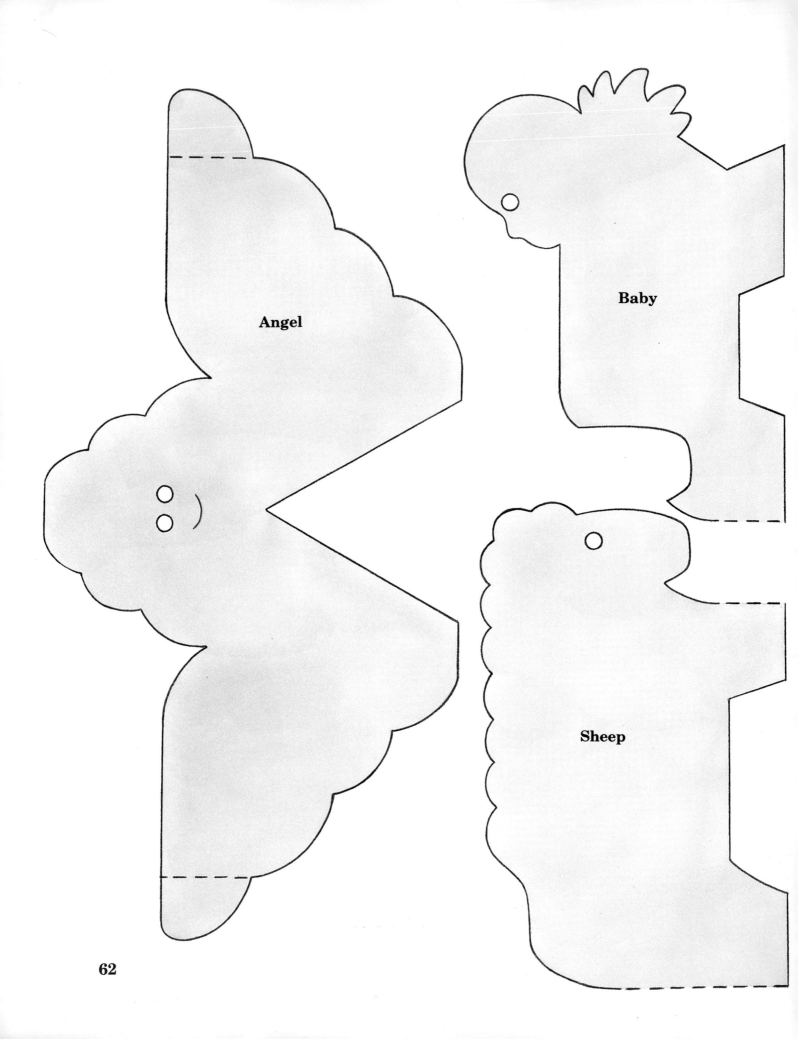

Angel

Baby

Sheep

62

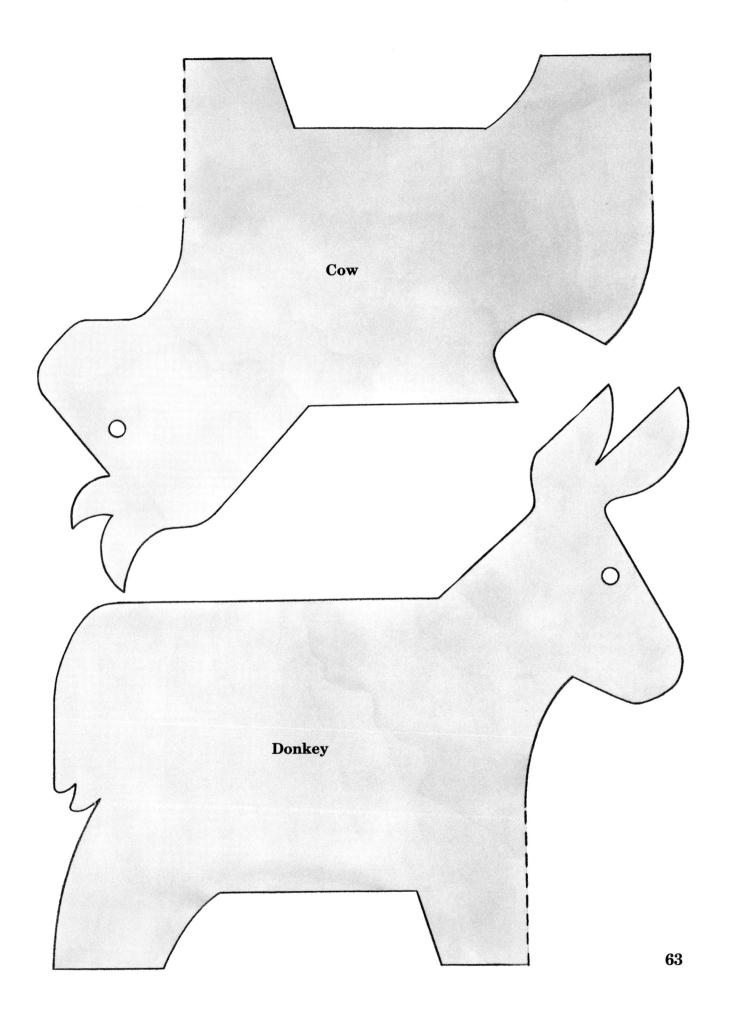

Cow

Donkey

63

Paper Heart Cluster

A heart-y touch makes these red-and-green paper ornaments. After you've finished one, you will want to make lots more to decorate the tree.

You will need:
Pencil
Tracing paper
Scissors
3½" x 7" piece of red paper
3½" x 7" piece of green paper
4" piece of metallic thread
Glue

1. Trace and cut out the pattern.

2. Cut out 2 heart flowers from the red paper and 2 from the green paper.

3. Fold 1 heart flower in half. Open the flower and fold it in half in the opposite direction.

4. Open the heart flower again. Now fold it in half diagonally.

5. Do this with the other 3 heart flowers. Open all the heart flowers.

6. To make the heart flower into a pocket, refold it as shown, so that the center creases of 2 opposite hearts meet in the middle. Press the heart pocket flat. Fold the other 3 heart flowers.

7. To make a hanger, fold the metallic thread in half to form a loop.

8. Line up the flat sides of 1 red and 1 green heart pocket. Glue the outside hearts together. Do the same thing with the other heart pockets. Then glue the 2 red-and-green sections together with the loop between them.

9. Place the glued heart flower cluster under a heavy book until the glue is dry.

10. Open the cluster as shown and glue the 2 remaining ends together.

Heart Flower

Fold line

Fold line

Fold line

GLUE

65

Cork Reindeer

With corks and chenille stems, you can make an entire team of red-nosed reindeer to prance and dance across the sky—or across your mantel and Christmas tree.

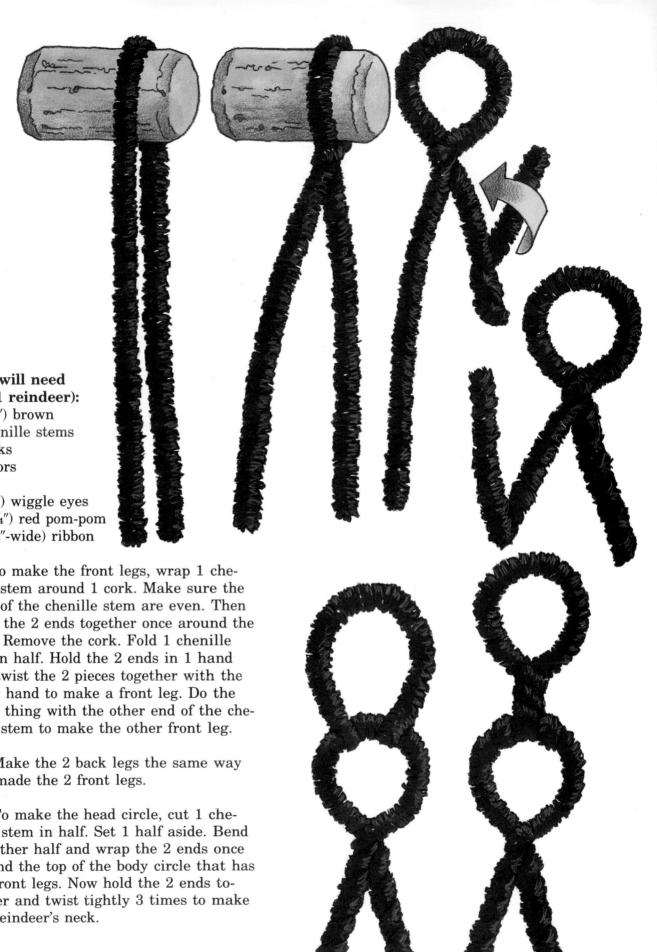

You will need (for 1 reindeer):
4 (12″) brown chenille stems
2 corks
Scissors
Glue
2 (½″) wiggle eyes
1 (1¼″) red pom-pom
7″ (⅜″-wide) ribbon

1. To make the front legs, wrap 1 chenille stem around 1 cork. Make sure the ends of the chenille stem are even. Then twist the 2 ends together once around the cork. Remove the cork. Fold 1 chenille end in half. Hold the 2 ends in 1 hand and twist the 2 pieces together with the other hand to make a front leg. Do the same thing with the other end of the chenille stem to make the other front leg.

2. Make the 2 back legs the same way you made the 2 front legs.

3. To make the head circle, cut 1 chenille stem in half. Set 1 half aside. Bend the other half and wrap the 2 ends once around the top of the body circle that has the front legs. Now hold the 2 ends together and twist tightly 3 times to make the reindeer's neck.

68

4. To make the antlers, fold 1 chenille stem in half with the ends even. Slip the stem through the top of the head circle and tightly twist the 2 halves together at the fold. Bend the antlers into a zigzag shape as shown.

5. Slip 1 cork through the body circle. Add the back legs. Slip the second cork into the head circle. If the cork is loose, twist the neck again.

6. Glue the wiggle eyes on the head cork. Glue the red pom-pom on the tip of the head cork for the nose. Tie the ribbon into a bow around the reindeer's neck.

Parachute Santa

Santa arrives in a most unusual style this Christmas— a delightful ornament or toy!

You will need:
Glue
Pom-poms: Red—1 (1″), 1 (1½″), 1 (5 mm);
  Black—2 (3 mm), 2 (5 mm); White—2
  (5 mm), 2 (7 mm)
Tracing paper
Pencil
Scissors
Scraps of felt: white, tan
16½″-square red bandanna
2 yards of cotton string
Large-eyed needle

1. Glue the 1″ and 1½″ red pom-poms together to form a head and body. Let dry.

2. Trace and transfer the patterns. Cut them out. From the tan felt, cut 1 face. From the white felt, cut 1 hatband.

3. To make the face, glue the tan circle to the center of the head. Glue the hatband across the top of the face. Glue 2 (3-mm) black pom-poms to the face for the eyes, and 1 (5-mm) red pom-pom for the nose. Glue 2 (5-mm) white pom-poms under the nose for a mustache. Glue 1 (7-mm) white pom-pom under the mustache for the beard and 1 just above the hatband for the top of the hat. Let dry.

4. Glue 2 (5-mm) black pom-poms down center of body for buttons. Let dry.

5. To make the parachute cords, cut 4 (16″) lengths of string. Wrap an end of 1 string 1″ from a corner of the bandanna and tie the string in a knot. Do this for each string.

6. Lay the bandanna flat and bring all 4 strings together so that the ends are even. Tie the strings together in a knot, 5″ from the ends.

7. Thread 2 string ends through the eye of the needle and poke the needle through the top of Santa's head just behind the hat. Remove the needle and tie these 2 ends to the remaining 2 string ends. Trim the ends close to the knot.

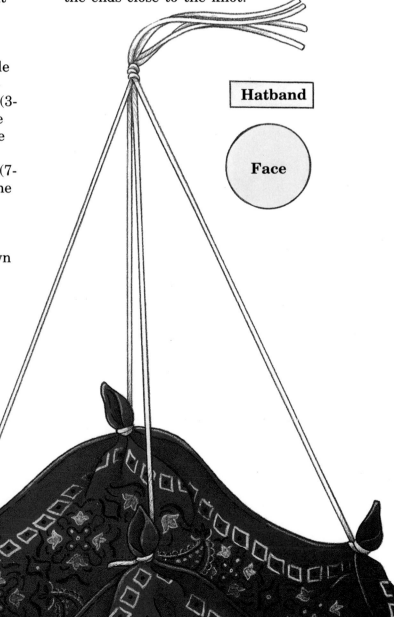

Hatband

Face

A Frame-Up

"I've been framed!" friends will shout when you give them their photos inside these colorful corrugated picture frames.

You will need:
Colored posterboard
Yardstick
Ruler
Pencil
Scissors
Glue
Photographs
Paper clips
Corrugated scalloped border
Scraps of corrugated fence border
Corrugated paper

Scalloped Frame

1. For a 5″ x 7″ photo, measure and mark a 7″ x 28″ rectangle on the back of the posterboard. Cut out the rectangle.

2. On the back of the rectangle, measure 4″ from 1 end. Draw a line all the way across the posterboard. Measure 10″ from this line and draw another line across. Then draw another line 10″ from the second line.

3. Fold and crease the posterboard along each line.

4. Unfold the rectangle. Find the center of the front of 1 of the 7″ x 10″ areas. Center the photograph in this area and glue it in place. Let the glue dry. With your ruler and pencil, measure and draw a line ½″ from the right and ½″ from the left side of the photograph.

5. Fold and crease the rectangle along the creased lines again. Glue the ends of the posterboard together where they overlap. Hold them in place with paper clips until they dry.

6. Cut 2 (11″) strips of the scalloped border. Glue 1 strip down each side of the frame on the lines.

7. Cut 1 (9½″) strip of the scalloped border for the top and 1 for the bottom of the frame. Place 1 strip across the top, lining up the scallops at the corners. Trim the corners of the side strips so that the scallop design continues around the corner of the frame. Do the same thing for the bottom strip. Glue the strips in place.

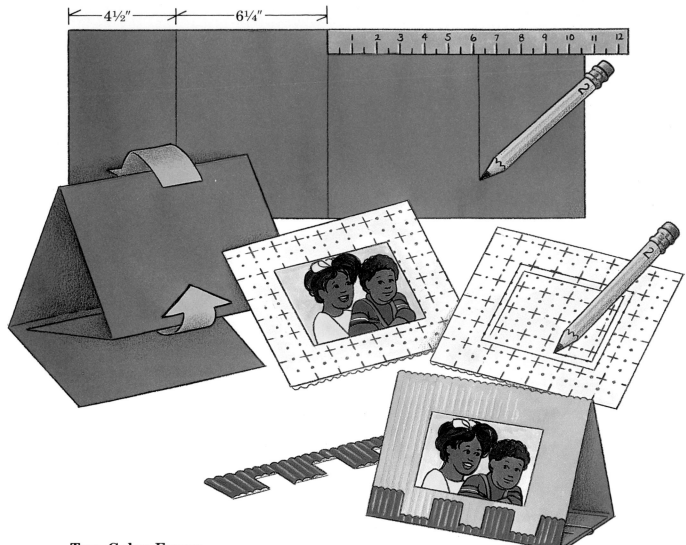

Two-Color Frame

1. For a 3½″ x 5″ or 4″ x 6″ photo, measure and mark an 8″ x 21½″ rectangle on the back of the posterboard. Cut it out.

2. Measure 4½″ from 1 end of the rectangle. Draw a line all the way across the posterboard. Measure 6¼″ from this line and draw another line across. Then draw another line 6¼″ from the second line.

3. Fold and crease the posterboard along each line. Glue the ends of the posterboard together where they overlap. Hold them in place with paper clips until dry.

4. Cut an 8″ x 6½″ rectangle from the corrugated paper.

5. On the back of the corrugated paper, place the photo in the center and trace around it. Inside this outline, draw another line following the next row of dots on the paper. Cut along this inside line to make a window for the photo.

6. Glue the corrugated paper frame to the front of the posterboard on 3 sides. Leave 1 side open so that the photo can be slipped in and out.

7. To decorate the frame, use scraps of the corrugated fence border strips. Glue the border strips to the front of the corrugated frame.

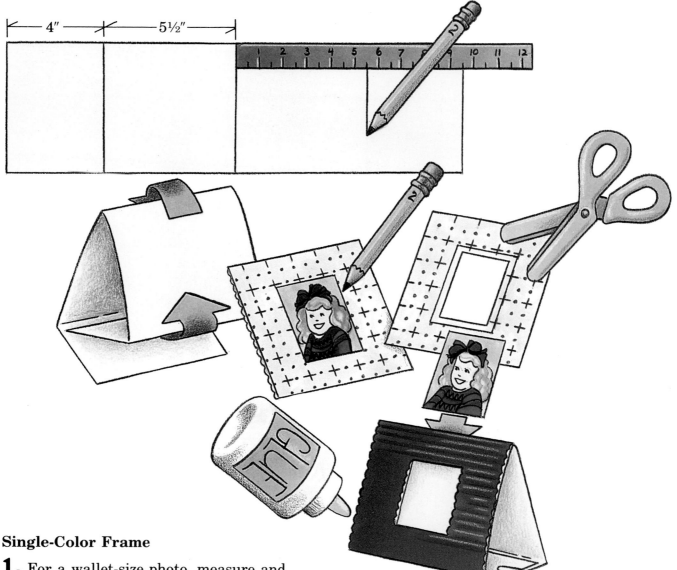

Single-Color Frame

1. For a wallet-size photo, measure and mark a 5½″ x 19″ rectangle on the back of the posterboard. Cut it out.

2. Measure 4″ from 1 end of the rectangle. Draw a line all the way across the posterboard. Measure 5½″ from this line and draw another line across. Then draw another line 5½″ from the second line.

3. Fold and crease the posterboard along each line. Glue the ends of the posterboard together where they overlap. Hold them in place with paper clips until they dry.

4. Cut a piece of corrugated paper that measures 5½″ x 5¾″.

5. On the back of the corrugated paper, place the photo in the center and trace around it. Inside this outline, draw another line following the next row of dots on the paper. Cut along this inside line to make a window for the photo.

6. Glue the corrugated paper frame to the front of the posterboard on 3 sides. Leave 1 side open so that the photo can be slipped in and out.

Porcupine Pincushion

What's the perfect pet for your favorite seamstress? A porcupine who's always on hand with needles and pins.

You will need:
Tracing paper and pencil
Scissors
Pop-up sponge (7⅜″ x 4″ x 1¾″)
Acrylic paint: pink, yellow
Round paintbrush
Small scrap of red felt
¼ yard (¼″-wide) red ribbon
Straight pins with colored heads

1. Trace and cut out the patterns. Trace the porcupine pattern onto the sponge. Cut out the porcupine with scissors.

2. Wet the sponge and watch it grow. Then let the porcupine dry.

3. Paint the face pink and let it dry. Then paint the body yellow. Let it dry.

4. Cut 1 ear from the felt. Fold the ear in half and pin it to the side of the head where it's marked on the pattern.

5. Tie the red ribbon into a small bow and pin it under the porcupine's chin.

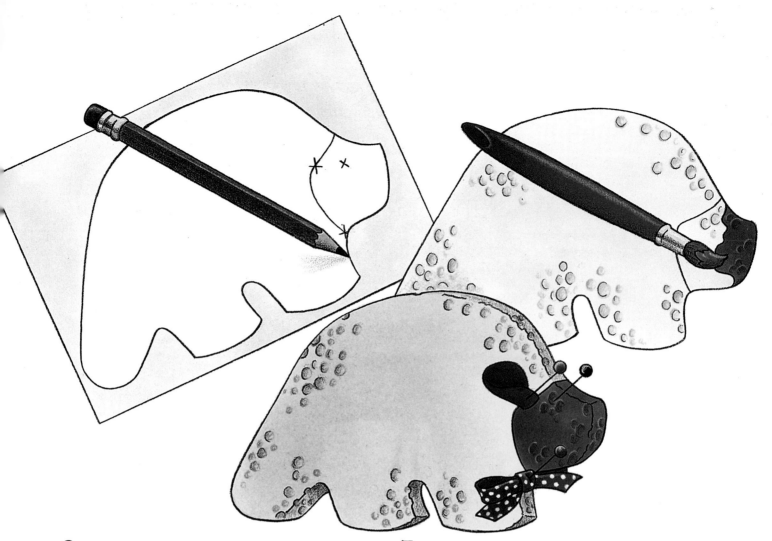

6. For the eye, stick a black-headed pin in the porcupine where it's marked on the pattern.

7. Stick straight pins with brightly colored heads into the porcupine for quills.

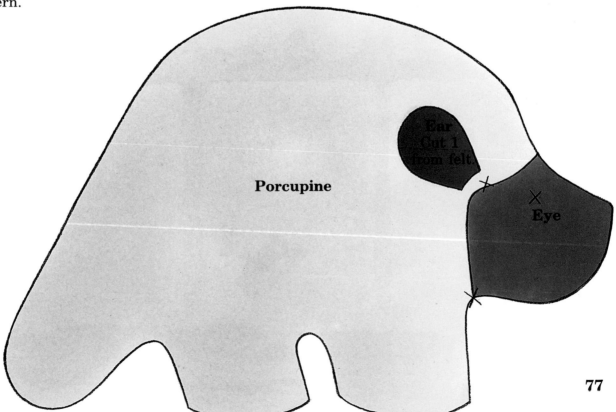

Porcupine

Ear
Cut 1
from felt

X
Eye

Herb Garden

Mary, Mary, what does your garden grow? Tasty herbs to give at Christmas to favorite cooks you know. There are chives and dill, rosemary and parsley, even oregano. And with gift tags and bows, these presents will be ready to go.

You will need:
A grown-up
Small pots or milk cartons with drainage
  holes
Small rocks or pebbles
Package of potting soil
Plastic plate and plastic bag
Herb seeds

1. Find a good indoor location for your plants. They should get 4 or 5 hours of direct sunlight every day. Check for drafts; you don't want to grow plants in a place where an air vent will blow on them. A warm, moist area is the best place to grow herbs. Temperatures of 70°-75° in the daytime and 65°-68° at night are a good general rule.

2. Check your container for a drainage hole. If it doesn't have 1, **have the grown-up** make a hole so that the soil won't stay too damp. Fill the bottom of the container with pebbles or small rocks. Then fill the container about ¾ full with potting soil. Put the plate under the pot.

3. Put the seeds in the container and cover them with soil, following the directions on the package. Some seeds need to be planted deeper than others. If you have any question though, it's always better to plant the seeds deeper. This helps the plants develop stronger roots. Now lightly water the soil.

4. Place the plastic bag over the container to help keep the seeds moist. Take the bag off for a few hours each day so that the seeds won't get moldy.

5. When the plants appear, take the bag off and throw it away. Water the plants. Then let the soil dry out before watering again.

Annual herbs (those lasting only one season) will come up in about a week to ten days. Perennials (plants that come up year after year) are slower to start.

6. Add a gift tag and bow to the herb container, and it's ready to give.

Spray-Painted Tees

For far-out fun and fantastic fashions, spray-paint T-shirts. They'll be a hit with all your fashion-forward friends.

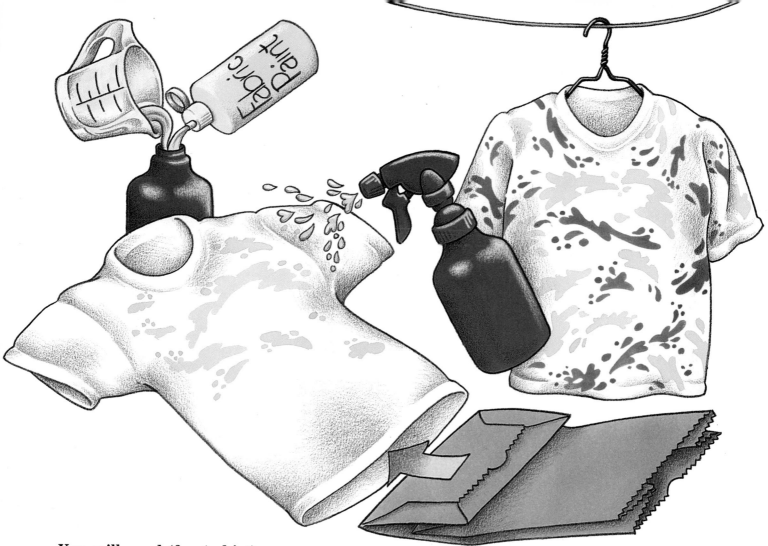

You will need (for 1 shirt):
Shiny fabric paint: 1 ounce of each color
Spray bottles (1 for each paint color)
Measuring cup
Water
Newspaper
White T-shirt
Brown paper grocery sack
Coat hanger

1. Pour 1 ounce of paint and 3 ounces of warm water into a spray bottle. Cap the bottle and shake it to mix the paint and water. Do the same thing with the other paints that you want to use.

2. To see how the paint will look when you spray it, test your spray on the newspaper. Adjust the spray nozzle for different looks. A mist setting creates a fine spatter of paint. A stream setting gives you a bolder look.

3. If the weather is nice, this would be a good project to do outdoors. Cover the ground or work surface (if you're indoors) with newspaper. Line the sleeves and the inside of the T-shirt with the grocery sack to keep the paint from bleeding through from the front to the back. Then spray the front of the shirt with the desired colors, 1 color at a time. Let the front of the shirt dry. Then turn it over and spray the back.

4. Remove the sack and hang the shirt on the hanger until it's thoroughly dry.

5. When the paint is dry, put the shirt in the dryer and run it on the regular cycle for 15 minutes. This will set the paint.

81

Letter-Gator

This green gator is a great catchall for mail. Make one for your mom and dad. Then they can say, "Later, Letter-Gator," and let him hold things for awhile.

You will need:
A grown-up
47 craft sticks
Glue
Ruler
Craft knife
Newspaper
Medium green acrylic paint
Paintbrush
Felt-tip markers: black, light green
White index card

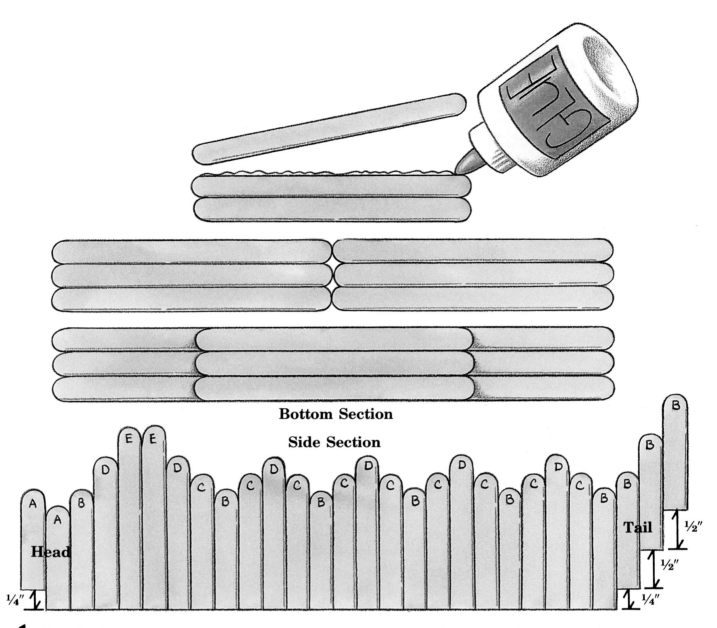

Bottom Section

Side Section

Head

Tail

1/4"

1/2"

1/2"

1/4"

1. For the bottom section of the gator, glue 3 craft sticks together, side by side. Make 2 more bottom sections. Place 2 sections end to end. Center and glue the remaining section on top.

2. Have the grown-up help you with this step. For the sides of the gator, you will need sticks cut in 5 different lengths. Cut the sticks by scoring them with the craft knife and then breaking them on the score line. You will need the following lengths: 4 (1½") As, 18 (1¾") Bs, 18 (2") Cs, 12 (2¼") Ds, 4 (2¾") Es.

3. Cover your worktable with newspaper. To make 1 side of the gator, start at the head and arrange the sticks side by side as shown. Line up the cut end of the second stick ¼" below the cut end of the first stick. Glue the sides of the sticks together. Line up the cut end of the next stick with the second stick. Glue the sides of the sticks together. Line up and glue 22 more sticks this way.

The last 3 sticks make the tail look like stairsteps, because each 1 moves up a little. Place the cut end of the first tail stick ¼" above the row. Glue it in place. Line up the cut end of the next stick ½" above this one and glue. Then line up the cut end of the last stick ½" above that one and glue it in place. Let the glue dry.

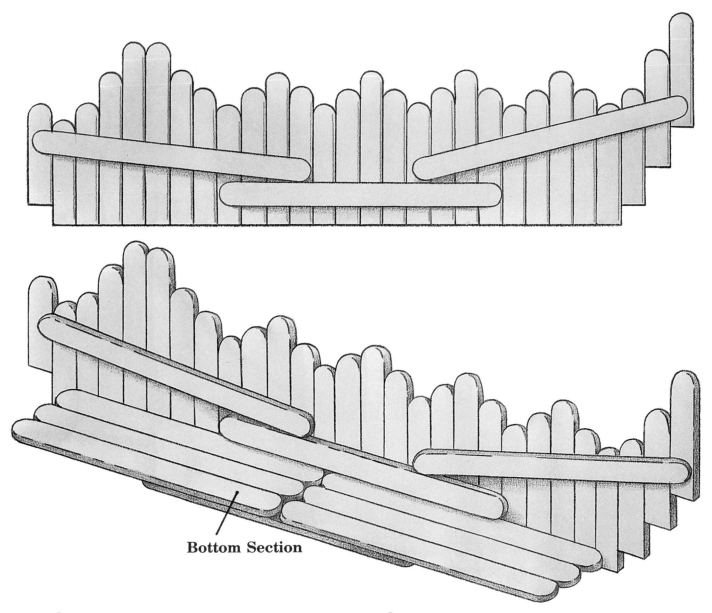

Bottom Section

4. To brace the side of the gator, glue 1 whole stick across the center of the side section ¼″ above the bottom edge. Glue a second stick to the right of the center 1, tilting it up on the right side so that it braces the last 3 sticks. Glue a third stick to the left of the center stick. Make sure all sticks in the side have some support.

5. Line up and glue the sticks side by side in the same order for the other side of the gator. Let the glue dry. Turn this side over and glue the support sticks on the back.

6. Glue the 2 sides to the bottom section of the gator. Make sure the support sticks on the side sections are facing each other. Prop the sides in place until the glue is dry.

84

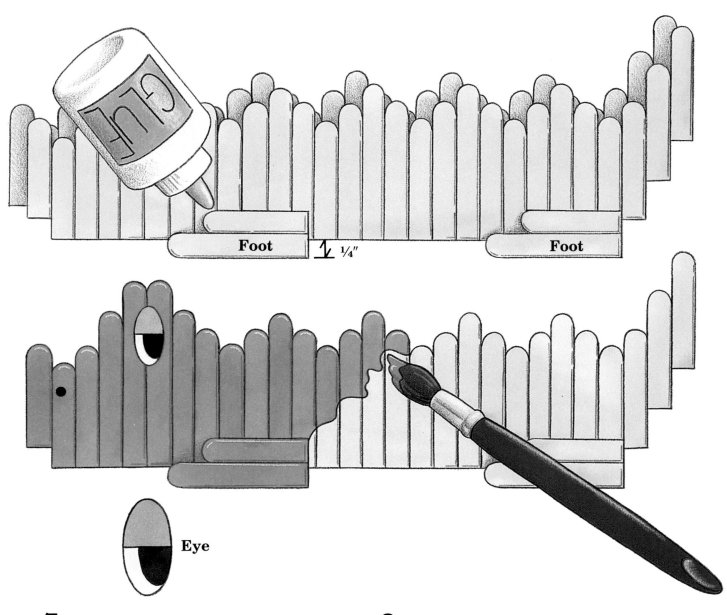

Foot

Foot

$\frac{1}{4}''$

Eye

7. **Have the grown-up** cut 4 (2″) sticks and 4 (1½″) sticks for the gator's feet. Take 1 (1½″) stick and 1 (2″) stick and line up the cut ends. Glue the sides together. For the other 3 feet, line up the sticks and glue them in the same way. Glue 2 feet to each side of the gator, letting the feet extend about ¼″ below the bottom section of the gator.

8. Paint the Letter-Gator medium green.

9. Trace and cut out the pattern for the eyes. Cut 2 eyes from the index card. With the light green marker, color the top of 1 eye; let dry. Draw a pupil with the black marker. Glue the eye to the side of the gator's head. Reverse the pattern and color the other eye. Glue it to the opposite side of the head. Look at the photo and draw the nostrils and a jagged mouth with the black marker.

85

Stamp It Out

Add pizzazz to plain paper with easy-to-make stamps. Just trace one of the designs here or make a special shape for a special friend.

You will need:
Pencil
Tracing paper
Small sharp scissors
Adhesive-backed latex foam padding for
   shoes
Hole punch
Small wooden blocks
Colored stamp pads
Stationery and envelopes
Black felt-tip marker

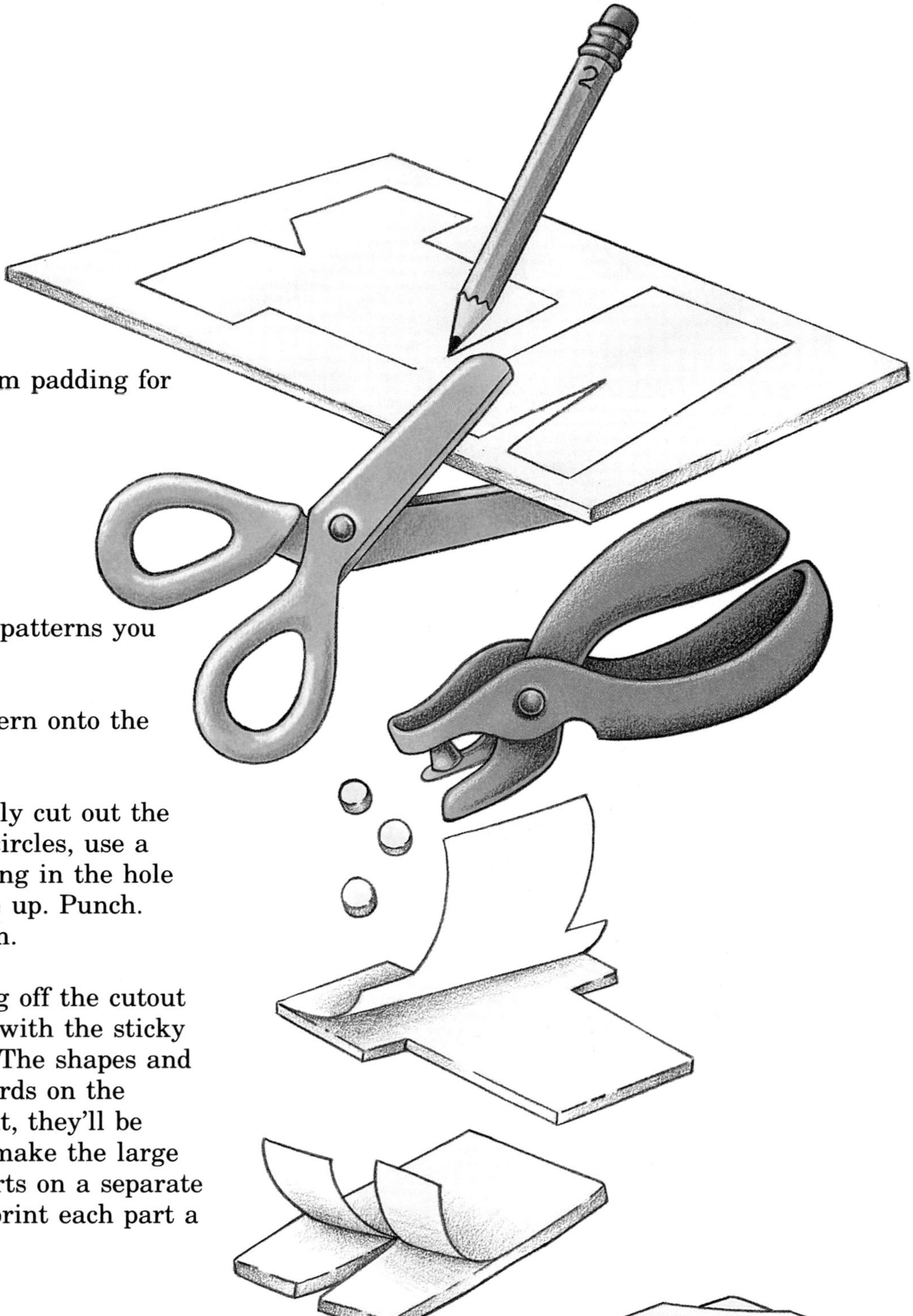

1. Trace and cut out the patterns you want to use.

2. Trace around the pattern onto the paper side of the padding.

3. Using scissors, carefully cut out the traced shapes. For small circles, use a hole punch. Put the padding in the hole punch with the paper side up. Punch. Trim away any extra foam.

4. Pull the paper backing off the cutout shapes. Place the cutouts with the sticky side down on the blocks. (The shapes and any words will be backwards on the blocks, but when you print, they'll be going the right way.) To make the large man, place each of his parts on a separate block. This way you can print each part a different color.

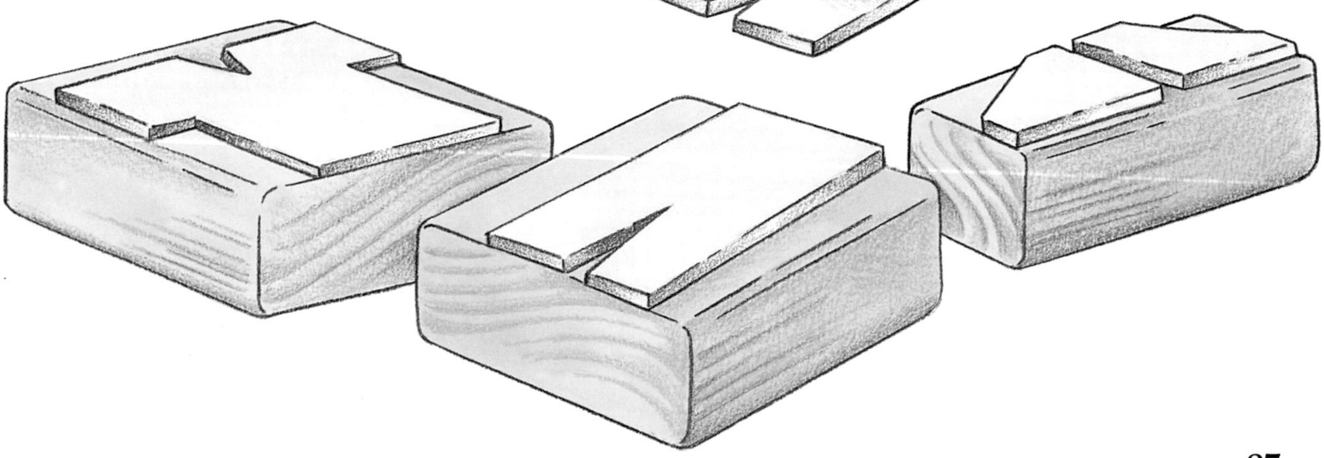

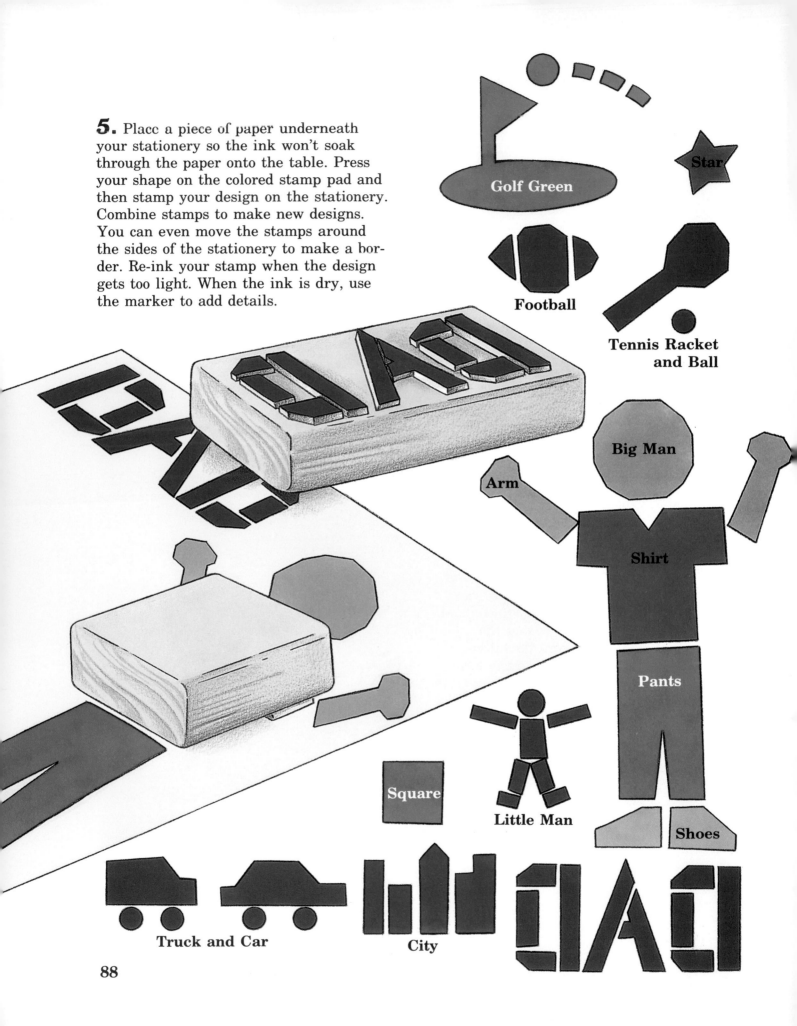

5. Place a piece of paper underneath your stationery so the ink won't soak through the paper onto the table. Press your shape on the colored stamp pad and then stamp your design on the stationery. Combine stamps to make new designs. You can even move the stamps around the sides of the stationery to make a border. Re-ink your stamp when the design gets too light. When the ink is dry, use the marker to add details.

Golf Green

Star

Football

Tennis Racket and Ball

Big Man

Arm

Shirt

Pants

Square

Little Man

Shoes

Truck and Car

City

88

Holiday Pins

Dazzle your friends with holiday pins! There are stars and a tree to wear at Christmas, a watermelon for the Fourth of July, and a spooky black cat for Halloween. Give them now and your friends will enjoy your gifts all year long.

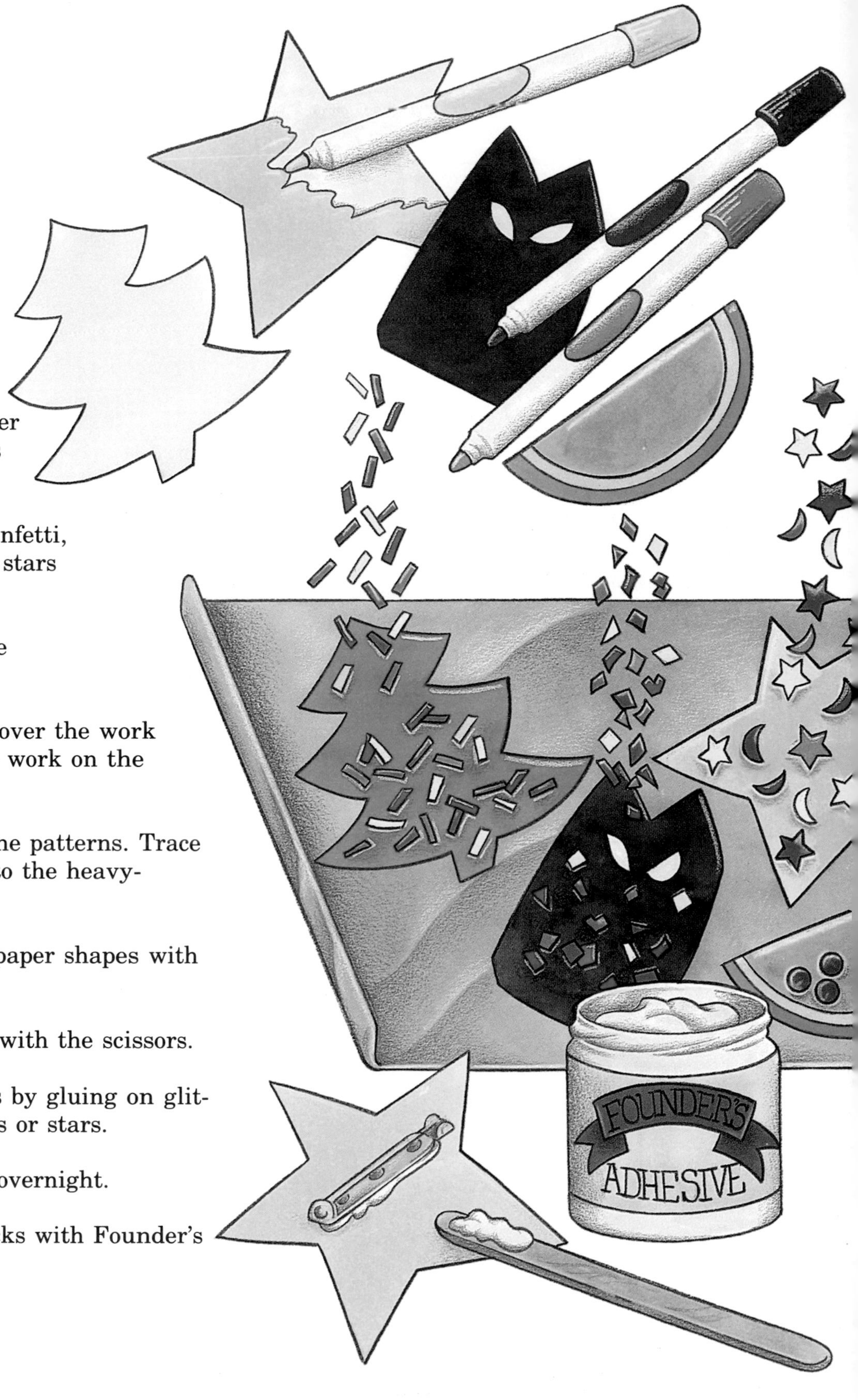

You will need:
Newspaper
Tracing paper
Pencil
White heavyweight paper
Colored felt-tip markers
Scissors
Cookie sheet
Glitter glue, metallic confetti,
   rhinestones, gummed stars
Glue
Pin backs
Founder's Adhesive glue
Craft stick

1. For easy clean-up, cover the work area with newspaper or work on the cookie sheet.

2. Trace and cut out the patterns. Trace around the patterns onto the heavy-weight paper.

3. Color 1 side of the paper shapes with the markers.

4. Cut out the shapes with the scissors.

5. Decorate the shapes by gluing on glitter, confetti, rhinestones or stars.

6. Let the shapes dry overnight.

7. Glue on the pin backs with Founder's Adhesive.

Star

Star

Star

Watermelon

Christmas Tree

Cat

91

Self-Portrait

Paint a portrait for a present—a self-portrait! Parents and grandparents will love having an original by you.

You will need:
Smock
Newspaper
Stretched artists' canvas (24″ x 36″)
Large and small bowls
Jar lid
Ruler
Pencil
Eraser
Easel
Acrylic paints
Paintbrushes (1 for each color)
¾″ vinyl tape for edge

1. Before you begin, put on the smock and cover the floor with newspaper.

2. With the pencil, lightly draw the shapes on the canvas. Trace around a bowl for the head. For the ears, trace half-way around the jar lid. Using the ruler, draw a square for the shirt and long rectangles for the pants legs. Draw triangles for the shoes. For the arms,

draw long rectangles. Trace around small bowl for the hands.

3. With the pencil, add the details to the face. Draw your hair, eyes, and smile. Draw yourself in your favorite outfit, or maybe in the uniform of your favorite ball team.

4. Draw any background details such as the sun, clouds, and grass. Round off the edges of any shapes that need to be curved. Erase all the extra lines. Make sure the canvas is free of eraser dust.

5. Set the canvas on the easel. To avoid smearing, paint your face first and move down the body. Then paint the background details. Let the paint dry.

6. To frame your self-portrait, cover the edges with the tape. Don't forget to sign and date your painting, too.

Parents' Workshop
Great Gifts for Children

Sock Hop Slippers

Don't get cold feet about what to give little friends. They will hop, skip, and jump through the house while these critters warm their toes!

You will need (for each pair):
Tracing paper
½ yard of fleece
1 yard of fusible web
½ yard of muslin
Water-soluble fabric marker

For the pig slippers:
¼ yard of pink striped fabric
Scrap of red fabric
Thread: dark pink, black
4 small black buttons
1 pair of red gripper socks
4″ (¼″-wide) elastic

For the frog slippers:
¼ yard of green pindot fabric
Thread: green, yellow, gold
4 (⅝″) sew-on wiggle eyes
1 pair of white gripper socks with green stripes

For the lamb slippers:
¼ yard of peach fabric
Scrap of blue pindot fabric
Thread: blue, peach
4 small blue buttons
1 pair of blue gripper socks

For the rabbit slippers:
¼ yard of blue pindot fabric
Thread: yellow, blue
4 small black shank buttons
½ yard (⅛″-wide) pink ribbon
2 (1″) white pom-poms
1 pair of yellow gripper socks

Note: You can make your own gripper socks by painting the bottoms of socks with slick fabric paint.

1. Trace and cut out the patterns needed. From the ¼ yard of fabric, cut 2 (6″ x 12″) rectangles. Cut 2 (6″ x 12″) rectangles each from the fleece, fusible web, and muslin. Using the fabric marker, transfer the pattern and markings twice to the right side of 1 fabric rectangle.

2. For the pigs: Pin the red fabric scrap, right side up, to a small piece of fusible web. Trace the cheek pattern on the fabric and cut out. Fuse the cheeks to the pig's face, following manufacturer's instructions. Repeat for second face.

3. For the lambs: Stack and pin the wrong side of the blue pindot to a small piece of fusible web. Transfer the patterns for the lamb's inner ears and nose to the fabric and cut them out. Referring to the pattern for placement, fuse the inner ears and the nose to the lamb's face. Repeat for the second face.

4. For all the designs: Stack 1 muslin rectangle, 1 fusible web rectangle, and the fabric rectangle with the faces (right side up). Fuse.

5. Stack the second fabric rectangle (wrong side up), fleece, and the animal face rectangle (muslin side down). Pin; then baste the layers together.

6. Using a narrow satin stitch, machine-appliqué any small fused shapes. Satin-stitch along the stitching lines indicated on the pattern, including the outer edges. Cut out the animal shape along the outside cutting edges, being careful not to cut into the stitching. Satin-stitch the outside edges again with a wider setting to fill in the stitches and cover the raw edges.

7. Stitch buttons, wiggle eyes, and ribbons to faces as indicated. Then stitch the faces to the top of the socks.

8. For the pig's tail: Cut a 2″ x 5″ rectangle from the pink striped fabric. Fold it in half lengthwise with right sides facing and raw edges aligned. Cut the elastic in half. Place 1 half on the tail, aligning 1 end of the elastic with 1 end of the fabric. Stitch, catching the end of the elastic in the seam. Continue stitching down the side but leave the other end open for turning. Clip the corners, turn, and press. Turn under ¼″ on the open end. Pull the elastic even with the open end and hold it while you sew the tail and elastic to the heel of the sock. Tack the tip of the tail in a curled position to the sock. Repeat for the other sock.

9. For the lamb's tail: Trace the tail pattern and add ¼″ seam allowances. Cut 4 tails from the peach fabric. With right sides facing, stitch 2 tails together, leaving an opening for turning. Clip seams, turn, and press. Turn under ¼″ on the open edges and tack the tail to the heel of the sock. Repeat for the other sock.

10. For the rabbit's tail: Tack a pompom to the heel of each sock.

Pig

Cheek

Rabbit

Frog

Lamb

Lamb's Tail

Inner Ear

Nose

98

Christmas Collars

No package will look as special this Christmas as a little girl bowed and beribboned in a holiday collar.

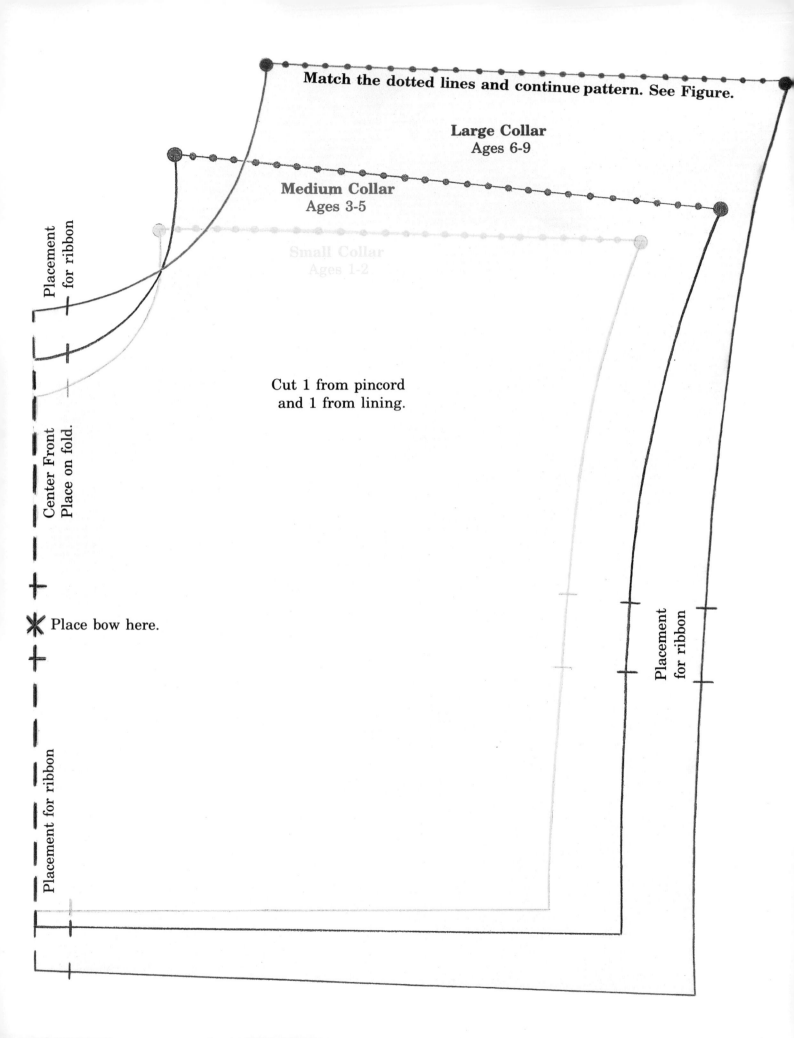

Match the dotted lines and continue pattern. See Figure.

Large Collar
Ages 6-9

Medium Collar
Ages 3-5

Small Collar
Ages 1-2

Placement for ribbon

Center Front
Place on fold.

Place bow here.

Cut 1 from pincord
and 1 from lining.

Placement for ribbon

Placement for ribbon

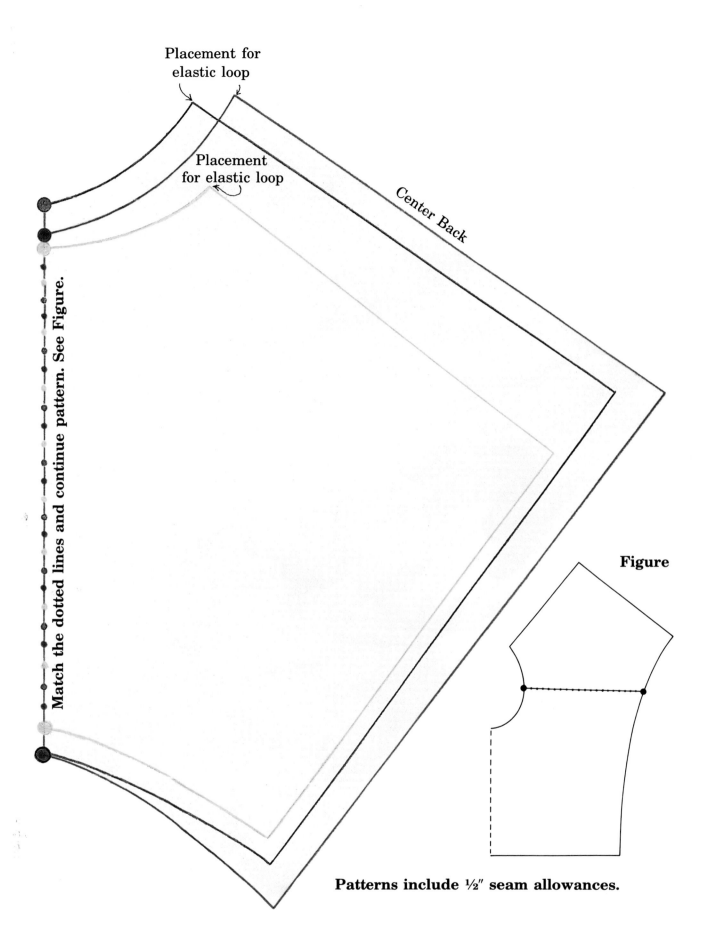

Placement for
elastic loop

Placement
for elastic loop

Center Back

Match the dotted lines and continue pattern. See Figure.

Figure

Patterns include ½″ seam allowances.

You will need (for 1 collar):

½ yard (45″-wide) white-on-white pincord or white piqué

½ yard (45″-wide) white batiste for lining

Water-soluble marker

¾ yard (¾″-wide) ribbon

Thread to match ribbon

2 elastic loops

White thread

¾ yard (1½″-wide) matching ribbon for bow

Liquid ravel preventer

Safety pin

½ yard (⅛″-wide) white ribbon

Note: The patterns include ½″ seam allowances.

1. Trace and transfer the pattern and all the markings.

2. Place the pattern on the fold of the collar fabric and cut out. With the water-soluble marker, transfer the markings. Repeat for the lining.

3. Pin the ¾″-wide ribbon to the right side of the collar between placement lines. Topstitch along all the long edges of the ribbons.

4. With raw edges aligned, pin the ends of 1 elastic loop to the right side of the collar along 1 straight edge at the top center back (loop will face to the inside). Stitch securely. Repeat with the second loop on the opposite side of the collar back.

5. With right sides facing and raw edges aligned, stitch the collar and lining together, leaving 1½″ open on 1 side. Trim seams to ¼″ and clip curves and corners. Turn and press. Slipstitch the opening closed.

6. Tie a bow with the 1½″-wide ribbon. Notch the ends of the ribbon. Then apply liquid ravel preventer to the ribbon ends. Safety-pin the bow to the center front of the collar.

7. To secure the collar around the neck, thread the ⅛″-wide white ribbon through the 2 elastic loops and tie it in a bow.

102

Frog Santa Sweatshirt

The kids will leap into the Christmas spirit as they hop into this Frog Santa sweatshirt.

You will need:
Tracing paper
3 (12″) squares of acetate
Permanent marker
Cutting board
Craft knife
Shiny fabric paint: green, red, black
3 paper plates
Sweatshirt
Paper grocery sack
Masking tape
3 sponges
1 (10-mm) jingle bell
White thread
Needle
2 (20-mm) sew-on wiggle eyes

1. Trace the design onto tracing paper.

2. Place the traced design under a sheet of acetate and trace the frog body (the green areas) with the permanent marker. Place the acetate on the cutting board. Cut along the marked lines with the craft knife. Set this stencil aside. Place another sheet of acetate on top of the design and trace the hat, mouth, scarf, and mittens (the red areas) with the permanent marker. Cut out. Set this stencil aside. Place the third sheet of acetate on top of the design and trace the fur outline, nose, and boots (the black areas). Cut out.

3. Pour the fabric paint onto the paper plates. (Use a different plate and sponge for each color.) Line the sweatshirt with the paper grocery sack. Lay the sweatshirt flat and tape the stencil for the frog body (green areas) in the center of the shirt; be sure to allow room for the hat at the top.

4. Using a sponge, apply the green paint to all the cutout areas. Let the paint dry before removing the stencil.

5. Position the stencil for the hat, mouth, scarf, and mittens (red areas). Tape the stencil down and sponge on the red paint as above. Let the paint dry before removing the stencil.

6. Position the stencil for the fur outline, nose, and boots (black areas). Tape the stencil down and sponge on the black paint. Let the paint dry before removing the stencil.

7. Using the white thread, sew the jingle bell on the tip of the hat.

8. Sew on the wiggle eyes.

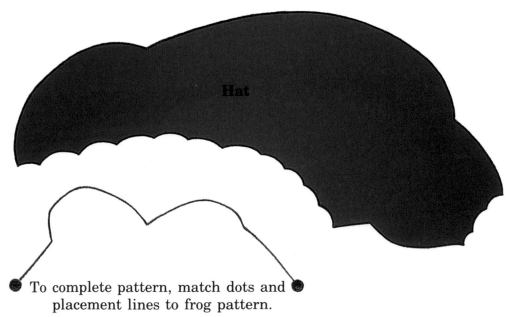

To complete pattern, match dots and placement lines to frog pattern.

Fur

Nose

Mouth

Boot

105

SS Teddy Towel

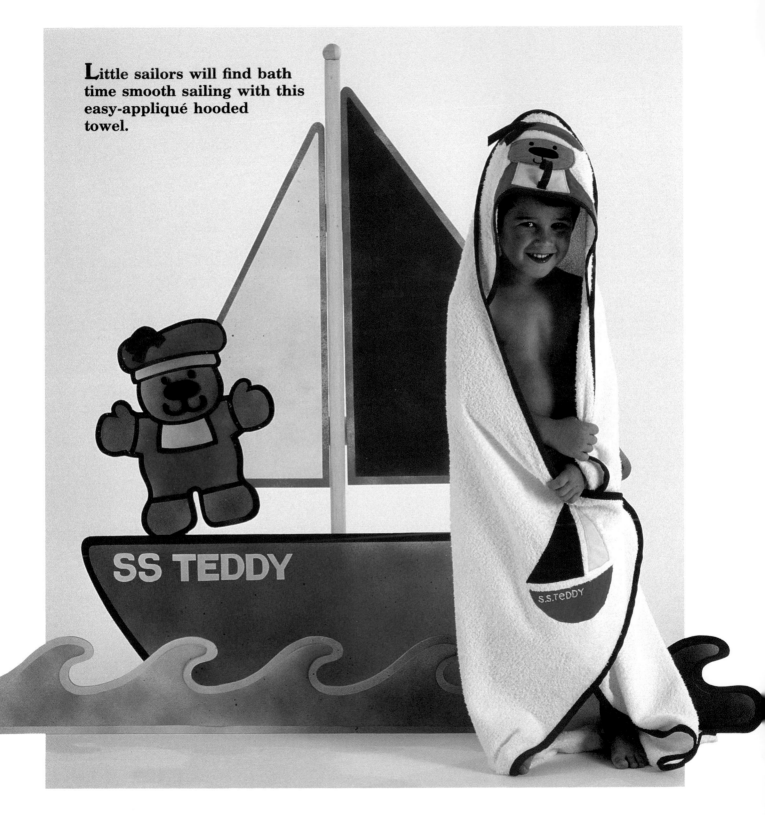

Little sailors will find bath time smooth sailing with this easy-appliqué hooded towel.

SS TEDDY

S.S.TeDDY

You will need:

12″ squares of red, blue, yellow, and tan cotton fabric

Scrap of black fabric

1⅝ yards (45″-wide) white terry cloth

6 yards (1″-wide) red double-fold bias tape

Thread to match fabrics

Embroidery floss: black, yellow

Embroidery needle

8″-square washcloth

1. Transfer the patterns for the appliqué pieces. Cut the pieces from the fabrics as marked.

2. For the towel, cut a 40″ square and a 16″ square from the terry cloth. For the hood, cut the 16″ square in half diagonally. Use 1 triangle for the hood and set the other aside.

3. Bind the long edge of the hood triangle with bias tape. Pin the bear appliqué pieces to the hood. (See pattern for placement.) Machine-appliqué them with matching thread in the following order: shirt, collar, face, paws, hatband, hat, and nose.

4. Using 3 strands of black floss, satin-stitch the bear's eyes and chainstitch the mouth. Cut a 12″ piece of the bias tape and topstitch the long edges together. From this piece, cut an 8″ strip for the hat decoration. Fold it in half widthwise and stitch the fold to the hat (see photo above). With the remaining 4″ piece of bias tape, make a loop for the washcloth. Fold under ¼″ on each end of the bias tape. Stitch 1 end to the center top of the collar and 1 to the center bottom.

5. Baste the hood, right side up, to 1 corner of the towel. Bind the edge of the towel with bias tape.

6. Place the towel with the bear appliqué face up at the top. Flip the lower left corner to the front (see photo at left) and pin the sailboat appliqué pieces to the top layer only. Machine-appliqué, using matching thread. To personalize the towel, chainstitch your child's name on the boat, using 3 strands of yellow floss.

7. Fold and pull the washcloth through the loop on the bear's collar for a bow tie.

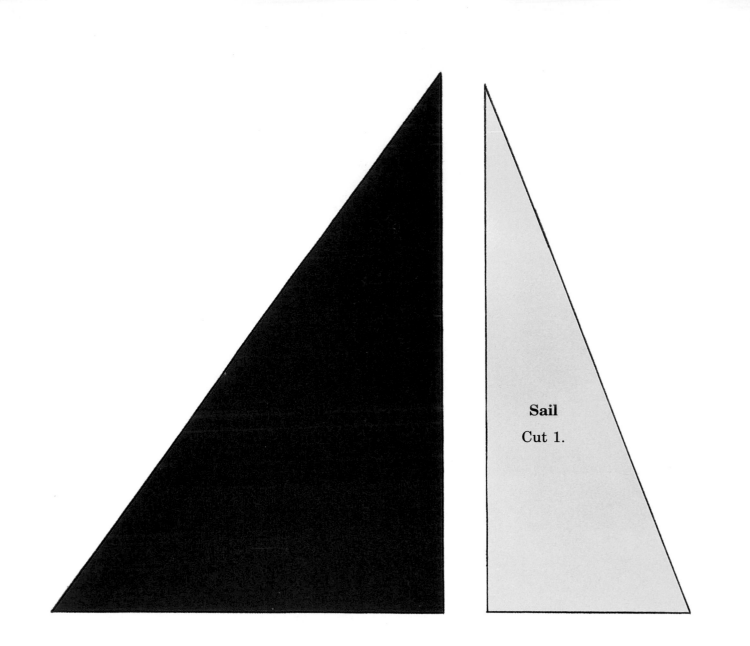

Sail
Cut 1.

S.S. TEDDY

Sailboat
Cut 1.

108

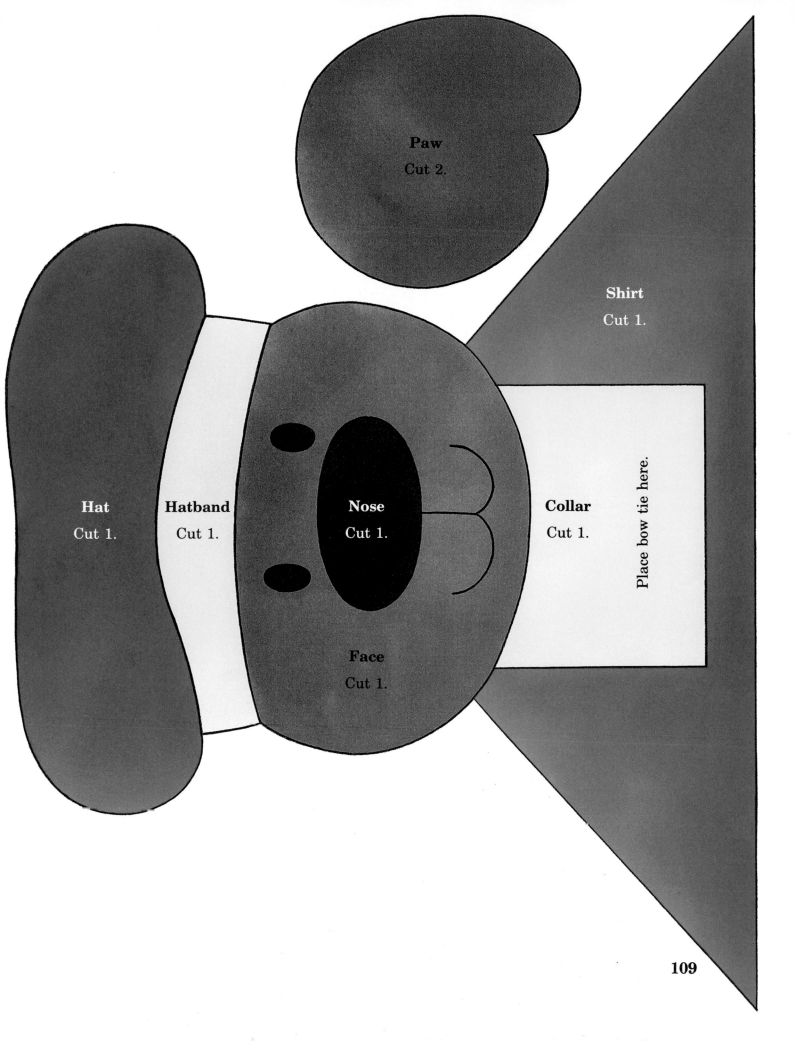

Paw
Cut 2.

Shirt
Cut 1.

Hat
Cut 1.

Hatband
Cut 1.

Nose
Cut 1.

Collar
Cut 1.

Place bow tie here.

Face
Cut 1.

109

Cross-stitched Longjohns

Giggling girls will find these cross-stitched longjohns perfect pajama-party attire. And you'll find the designs quick and easy to stitch on the waffle-weave grid.

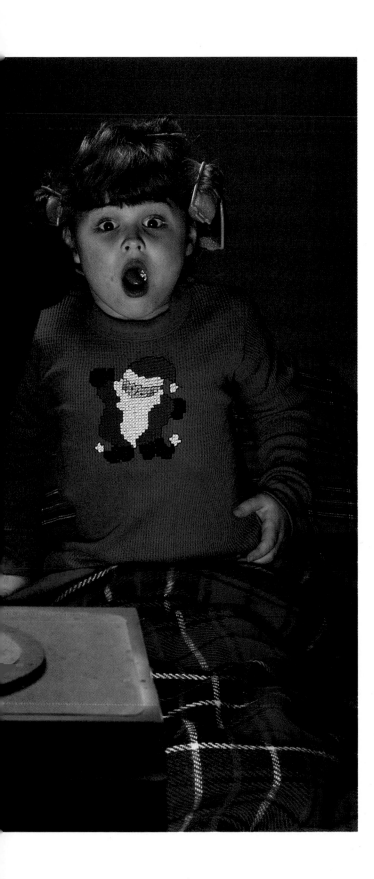

You will need:
Thermal shirt
Water-soluble marker
DMC embroidery floss: For Santa—321,
 white, 310, 948, 760; For Bear—321,
 910, 676, 310
Crewel needle
Lightweight fusible interfacing

1. Wash and dry the thermal shirt.

2. Find the center front of the shirt
neckline by folding the shirt in half. With
the water-soluble marker, mark the center front. Count down 7 rows below the
center mark and mark the square. Begin
stitching the top of the design at this
point (see graph).

3. To ensure smooth stitches, separate
all the strands and put them back together before threading the needle. Cross-
stitch directly on the shirt, using all 6
strands. (It isn't necessary to use waste
canvas.) Follow the grid in the knit and
make 1 cross-stitch over each square.

4. To protect the back of the cross-stitch
design, follow the manufacturer's instructions to iron a piece of fusible interfacing
to the wrong side of the design, covering
the stitches.

Color Code

DMC (used for sample)

Step 1: Cross-stitch
(6 strands)

◼	321 Christmas Red
▨	910 Emerald Green-dk.
▨	676 Old Gold-lt.
	White
▨	310 Black
▨	948 Peach-vy. lt.
▨	760 Salmon

Step 2: Backstitch
(4 strands)

310 Black

Step 3: French Knots
(4 strands)

● 310 Black
● 321 Christmas Red

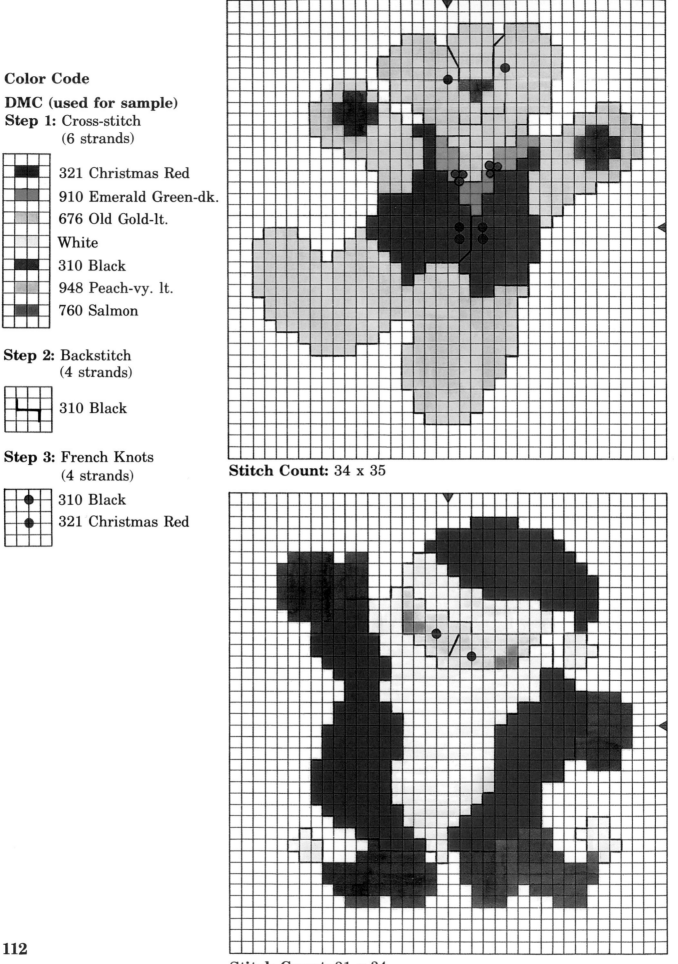

Stitch Count: 34 x 35

Stitch Count: 31 x 34

112

Muffler, Mittens, and Cap

When your little ones take off in search of Santa and the North Pole, you can be sure they're toasty warm in this coordinated set.

NORTH POLE

MAP

You will need:

Sizes 2, 3, and 5 knitting needles (or size to obtain gauge)

Size 5 (24″) circular knitting needle

Sportweight yarn: 6 oz. red, ½ oz. each of blue and green

Tapestry needle

Stitch markers

Stitch holder

Standard Knitting Abbreviations

st(s)—stitch(es)

St st—stockinette stitch (k 1 row, p 1 row)

k—knit

p—purl

beg—begin(ning)

rep—repeat(ing)

dec—decrease(s)

tog—together

rem—remain(ing)

inc—increase(s)

Finished sizes: Cap is a child's medium. Mittens are child's small (approximately 8″ in length). Changes for child's medium (8½″ in length) and large (9″ in length) are in parentheses. Scarf is approximately 30″ long and 5″ wide.

Gauge: 13 sts and 13 rows = 2″ in St st on largest needles.

Note: When changing colors, remember to wrap old yarn over new so that no holes occur. When sewing seams, be sure to align pattern rows. Scarf can be made longer or shorter by adding or subtracting stitches in multiples of 4.

Cap: With smallest needles and red, cast on 132 sts. Work in k 1, p 1 ribbing for 2″. Change to largest needles and work 2 rows in St st. *Next row:* Work according to row 1 of chart, rep pattern as indicated. After row 36 of chart, cut blue and green. With red, work 2 rows in St st. Work dec rows as follows: *Row 1* (right side): * K 6, k 2 tog, rep from * across. *Row 2 and following even-numbered rows:* P across. *Row 3:* (K 5, k 2 tog) across. *Row 5:* (K 4, k 2 tog) across. *Row 7:* (K 3, k 2 tog) across. *Row 9:* (K 2, k 2 tog) across. *Row 11:* (K 1, k 2 tog) across. *Row 13:* K 2 tog across, end with k 1. *Row 14:* P across rem 17 sts. Cut yarn, leaving a tail. Thread tail through rem sts, pull up tightly, and secure. Sew seam. Weave in yarn ends. Make a pom-pom with red yarn and attach to top of cap.

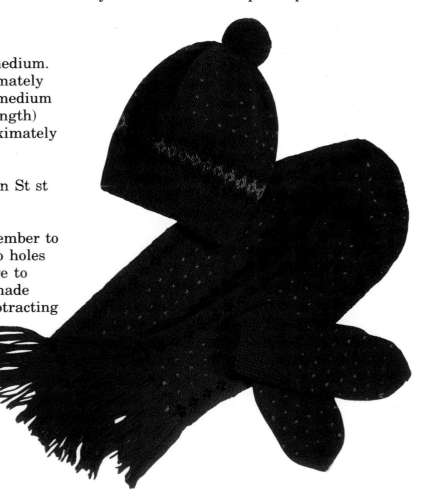

Mittens: Make 2. With medium-size needles and red, cast on 42 (46, 46) sts and work in k 1, p 1 ribbing for 2½". Change to largest needles and work according to rows 12-36 of chart, rep pattern as indicated. After 6 (8, 8) rows in pattern, beg shaping thumb as follows: *Row 1* (right side): K 20 (22, 22) in pattern, slip a marker on needle, inc 1 in each of next 2 sts, slip a marker on needle, k 20 (22, 22) in pattern. *Note:* Do not work color pattern on thumb sts; carry green across. *Row 2:* P across. *Row 3:* K to first marker, inc 1 in st after marker, k to st before 2nd marker, inc 1 in st before marker, k to end of row. Rep rows 2 and 3 until there are 10 (12, 14) sts between markers. P 1 row. *Next row:* K to first marker, place next 10 (12, 14) sts on holder for thumb, cast on 2 sts, k rem sts. Continue working in pattern until mitten measures 7" (7½", 8") from beg. Cut green and work dec rows with red in St st as follows: *Row 1* (right side): * K 4 (5, 6), k 2 tog, rep from * across. *Row 2:* P across. *Row 3:* * K 3 (4, 5), k 2 tog, rep from * across. Rep rows 2 and 3 (working 1 st fewer between dec) 2 (3, 4) times. *Next row:* K 2 tog across = 7 (7, 6) sts rem. Cut yarn, leaving a tail. Thread tail through rem sts, pull up tightly, and secure. *Thumb:* Slip thumb sts from holder onto size 5 needles and join red. Cast on 2 sts at beg of each of the next 2 rows and work in St st on 14 (16, 18) sts for 1½" (2", 2"). Cut yarn, leaving a tail. Thread tail through all sts, pull up tightly, and secure. Sew thumb seam. Sew mitten seam. Weave in yarn ends.

Scarf: With size 5 circular needle and red, cast on 191 sts. *Rows 1 and 2:* K 1, p 1 across. *Row 3* (right side): K across. *Row 4:* P across. *Rows 5-7:* Work rows 1-3 of chart, rep pattern as indicated. *Rows 8 26:* Work rows 12-30 of chart. *Rows 27-29:* Work rows 1-3 of chart. *Row 30:* P across. *Row 31:* K across. *Rows 32 and 33:* K 1, p 1 across. Bind off in p. Weave in yarn ends. Cut 4 (9") strands of red for each tassel. Knot 11 tassels across each end of scarf.

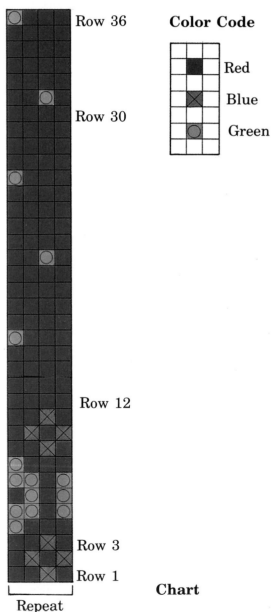

Row 36

Row 30

Color Code

Red

Blue

Green

Row 12

Row 3

Row 1

Chart

Repeat

Storybook Headboards

Dreams will blossom in the nursery when you combine simple carpentry and painting to produce these story-book headboards.

You will need (for 1 headboard):
Yardstick
2 (48") newel posts
Electric drill and ¾" bit
Saber saw or band saw
48" (1") wooden dowel
Wood glue
2 (6-foot) pine or fir 1 x 2s
8 (1" x ½") corner irons with screws
T-square
2 (10-foot) grade-C pine 1 x 4s
Tracing paper
Sandpaper: medium, fine grade
Latex primer
3-penny finishing nails
Wood filler
White semi-gloss latex paint
Clear acetate for stencils
Craft knife
Acrylic paints: pink, light green for
    flowers; yellow, white, blue, black for
    cow and moon
Paintbrushes
Clear varnish

Making the Headboard

1. Mark the center of 1 side of each newel post 6½" from the bottom edge. Using the electric drill and bit, drill a 2"-deep hole at each mark. Cut a 37" length of dowel with the saber saw or band saw. Fill the drilled holes with wood glue and insert the dowel between the 2 posts. Let dry.

2. Cut 2 (33¼"-long) pieces of 1 x 2 pine or fir. Attach the pieces between the posts as shown. (See Figure.) Lay the frame flat while the glue dries. Check for right angles at the corners with the T-square.

3. From each 10-foot pine 1 x 4, cut 2 (31") lengths and 2 (29") lengths. Cut 2 (29") lengths from the 1 x 2 pine or fir.

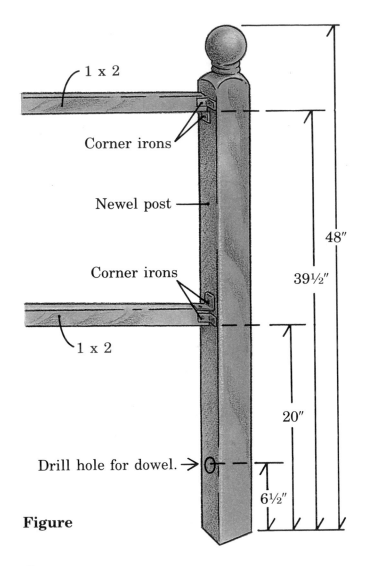

1 x 2

Corner irons

Newel post

Corner irons

1 x 2

Drill hole for dowel.

48"

39½"

20"

6½"

Figure

4. Lay the slats side by side on the frame, with the longer ones in the center and the 1 x 2 slats on the outside. Align the slats along the bottom edge. Enlarge, trace, and transfer the curve pattern. Center and trace the curve across the top edge of the slats.

5. Trace and transfer the star or heart cutout pattern, placing the top of the pattern 3" from the top edge of the 2 center boards.

6. Cut the curve and cutout, using the saber or band saw.

7. Sand each piece and coat with the primer.

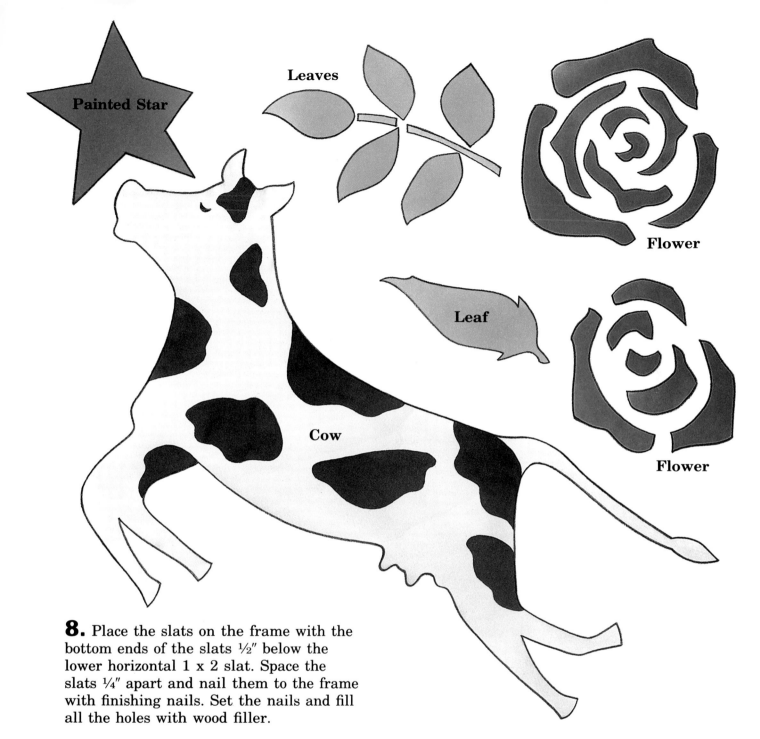

Painted Star

Leaves

Flower

Leaf

Cow

Flower

8. Place the slats on the frame with the bottom ends of the slats ½″ below the lower horizontal 1 x 2 slat. Space the slats ¼″ apart and nail them to the frame with finishing nails. Set the nails and fill all the holes with wood filler.

Finishing the Headboard

1. Paint the entire headboard with the semi-gloss latex paint. Let dry. If necessary, apply a second coat and let dry.

2. To make the stencils, lay a piece of acetate over each desired pattern. With a ballpoint pen, trace the pattern. Cut it out, using the craft knife.

3. Use the flower and leaf stencils to create your own design. Paint the design with acrylic paints, referring to the photograph for colors and placement. Let dry.

4. Coat the painted headboard with the clear varnish.

119

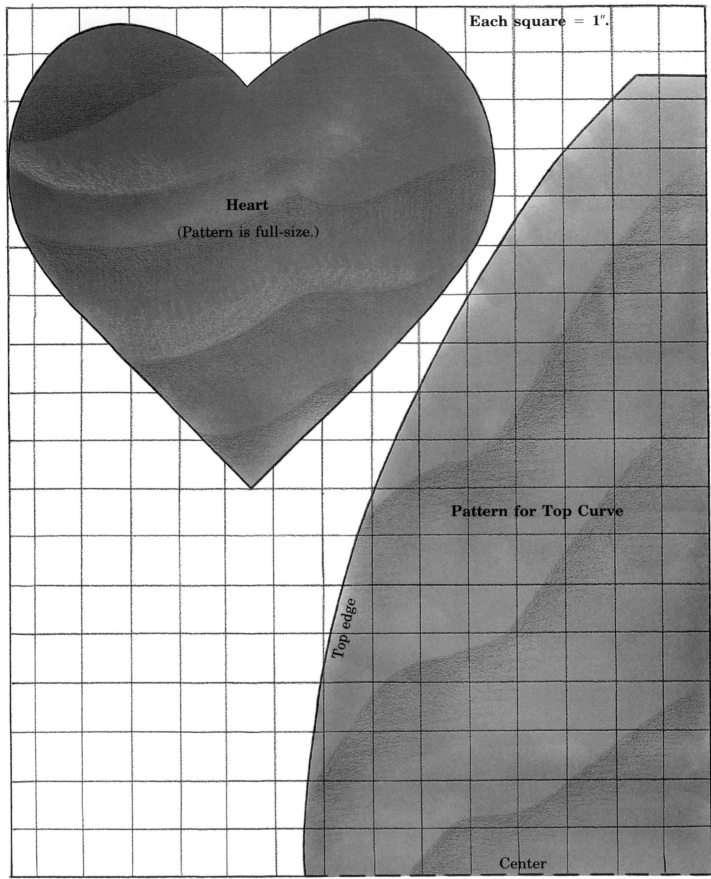

Each square = 1″.

Heart

(Pattern is full-size.)

Pattern for Top Curve

Top edge

Center

Place pattern on fold line.

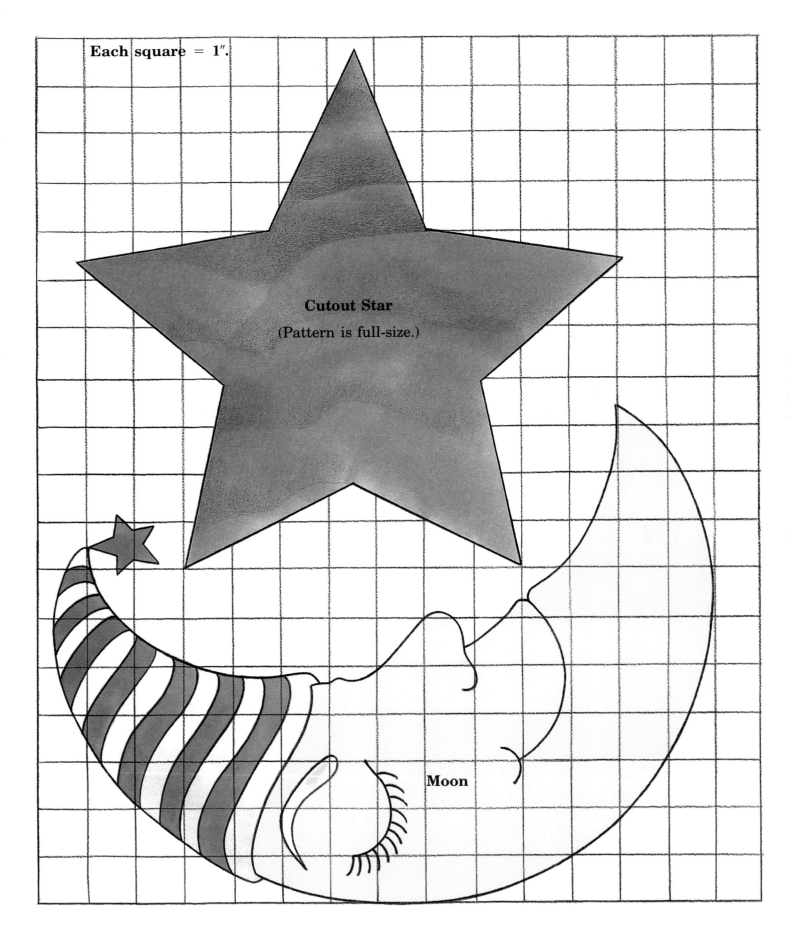

Each square = 1".

Cutout Star

(Pattern is full-size.)

Moon

Rock-a-bye Baby

Here's a peachy idea for the little girl on your Christmas list. It's a doll cradle made from two peach baskets. It's bound to conjure up magic in the nursery for her and her babies.

You will need:
Pliers
2 (12″ x 18″) peach baskets
Handsaw or coping saw
Scissors
Hot-glue gun and glue sticks
1 (30″-long) pine 1 x 4
Band saw or saber saw
4-penny finishing nails
1 (10″-long) 1 x 2 for crosspiece
Sandpaper

White spray paint
1 yard (45″-wide) fabric for basket lining
2 yards (2″-wide) gathered cotton trim
¾ yard (54″-wide) decorative fabric for bow and edging
Sewing thread
Fabric stiffener
Wax paper

Making the Cradle

1. Use the pliers to remove the wire handles from both baskets.

2. To make the cradle bonnet, measure 9″ from the end of 1 basket and draw a line all the way around underneath the basket. Cut on the line, using the handsaw to cut through the side rim and scissors to cut the lattice strips.

3. Glue the bonnet section to the inside rim of the other basket.

4. Trace and transfer the rocker pattern to the 1 x 4. Cut 2, using the band saw. If necessary, contour the top edge of the rocker to fit the bottom of the basket.

5. To make the cradle base, center and nail 1 rocker to each end of the 1 x 2 crosspiece, aligning the top edges. Sand the rough edges.

6. Glue the base to the basket. Paint the entire piece. Let dry.

Making the Lining and Trim

1. Cut 10″-wide strips from the lining fabric, piecing as needed to make 3 yards. Finish 1 long edge with pinking shears or a narrow hem. Run a gathering thread along the other edge. Place the lining, gathered edge up and right side out, along the sides inside the cradle. Adjust the gathers to fit the rim. Wrap the edge of the lining over the rim of the basket, except in the bonnet area. Inside the bonnet area, let the lining stand up straight and glue the lining edge to the basket rim. (See photo.)

2. Measure around the front of the cradle from 1 edge of the bonnet to the other. Cut a piece of the gathered trim

this length plus 2″. Turn under 1″ at each end. Glue the wrong side of the unfinished edge of the trim over the edge of the lining on the outside of the cradle.

Measure the edge of the cradle inside the bonnet. Cut a piece of trim this length plus 2″. Turn under 1″ at each end. Glue the wrong side of the unfinished edge of the trim over edge of the lining.

3. For the edging, measure all the way around the outside of the cradle. Cut a 2″-wide strip of the decorative fabric this length plus 2″. Fold under ½″ along each long edge and press. Glue the wrong side of the strip around the rim of the cradle, covering the raw edges of the lining and trim. Turn under and overlap the ends.

Cut a second 2″-wide piece of decorative fabric the same length as the trim inside the bonnet area plus 2″. Fold under ½″ along each long edge and 1″ on each end and press. Glue the wrong side of the strip inside the bonnet area, covering the raw edges of the lining and the trim.

Making the Bow

1. Cut a 6″ x 40″ strip of decorative fabric. Turn under 1½″ along each long edge and press. Coat the strip with fabric stiffener. While it is still wet, glue this strip along the front edge of the bonnet, forming ripples down both sides. Trim the ends. (See photo.)

2. From the decorative fabric, cut a 26″ strip and a 20″ strip, both 8″ wide. Press under 2″ on each long edge. Cut a 4″ x 6″ piece. Press under 1″ along each long edge. Coat each strip with fabric stiffener.

While the strips are still wet, bring the raw ends of the 26″ strip together to make loops for the bow. Repeat with the 20″ strip and place it on top of the first strip. Pinch the loops in the center and wrap them with the 6″ strip. Shape and stuff the bow loops with wax paper to hold the shape while drying. Place the formed bow on wax paper to dry. Then glue the bow to the top of the cradle.

Making the Bedding

You will need:
12″ x 18″ x 2″ piece of foam
½ yard of quilted fabric
½ yard of white cotton fabric
⅓ yard (3″-wide) flat eyelet lace
⅓ yard (1″-wide) flat eyelet lace
Thread to match
Polyester stuffing
12″ x 14″ piece of striped flannel

1. For the mattress, cut 1 (9½″ x 15″) piece of foam to fit inside the basket. For the cover, cut 1 (18″ x 25″) piece of quilted fabric. Fold the fabric in half lengthwise with right sides facing. Stitch across 1 end and along the side. Clip the corners and turn. Insert the foam and stitch the end closed.

2. For the top sheet, cut a 12″ x 14″ piece of white fabric. With right sides facing and raw edges aligned, stitch the 3″-wide piece of eyelet to 1 (12″) end. Fold the lace back and press. Turn under ⅛″ on the raw edges and hem.

3. For the pillow, cut a 6″ x 7½″ piece of white fabric. Fold in half with 6″ sides aligned. Stitch 1 end and the long side. Turn, stuff and stitch the end closed.

4. For the pillowcase, cut a 6½″ x 8″ piece of white fabric. Stitch the 1″-wide eyelet to 1 (8″) edge, right sides facing and raw edges aligned. Fold the eyelet back and press. Fold the pillowcase in half, right sides together and 6½″ sides aligned. Stitch 1 end and the side, leaving

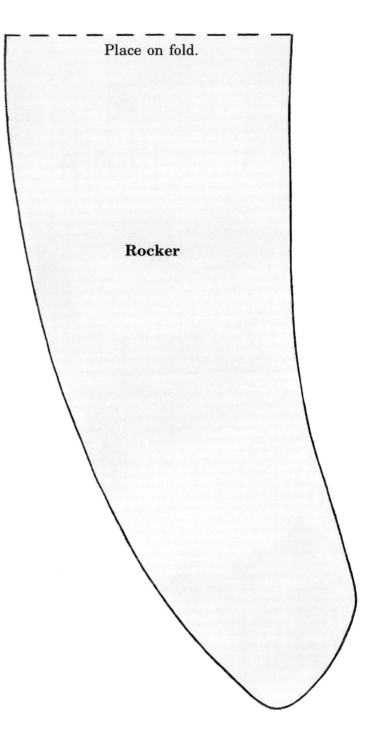

Place on fold.

Rocker

the eyelet-trimmed edge open. Turn right side out and slip the pillow inside.

5. For the blanket, hem the flannel on all sides.

Garden Glove Puppet

Naughty Peter Rabbit and his friends will keep little ones entranced as you tell stories of garden adventures with the help of this whimsical glove.

You will need:
Felt scraps: pink, red, blue, lavender,
  yellow, green, light green, tan, white
Hot-glue gun and glue sticks
Garden glove
4 (1″) white pom-poms
12 (½″) white pom-poms
4 (⅛″) pink pom-poms
10 (8-mm) black wiggle eyes
1 (1″) pink pom-pom
1 (1⅜″) woven straw hat
5 yellow seed beads
Yellow thread
4″ (1″-wide) white eyelet trim
8″ (⅛″-wide) pink satin ribbon

1. Trace the patterns and cut them out. Transfer the patterns to felt and cut them as marked.

2. To make a rabbit head, glue 1 (1″) white pom-pom to the palm side of a glove finger. Glue on ½″ white pom-poms for cheeks and a ⅛″ pink pom-pom for the nose. Then glue the wiggle eyes in place. Repeat for the other 3 rabbits.

3. To make Mr. McGregor, glue the 1″ pink pom-pom to the inside of the thumb. Glue on the mustache and wiggle eyes. Then glue on the straw hat. To finish Mr. McGregor, glue his hands to the back of his shirt. Glue the shirt and hands just below the head. Glue the pocket on the overalls and the overalls over the shirt.

4. For Peter Rabbit, glue the pockets to the vest. Sew on beads for buttons. Then glue the vest below Peter's head.

5. For Flopsy and Mopsy, cut 2 (2″) lengths of eyelet trim. Cut the pink satin ribbon in half and tie each piece in a bow. Glue the eyelet trims to the wrong side of the dresses on the bottom edge. Glue the collars in place on the dresses

and the bows to the collars. Glue the completed outfits below the heads.

6. To dress Cottontail, glue the knot on the bow tie and the bow tie below his chin.

7. For the garden, glue the row of short plants to the row of tall plants. Glue the plants across the palm of the glove. Glue the fence over the plants, lining up the lower edge of the fence with the lower edge of the plants.

8. To finish the rabbits, glue a pink inner ear to each white outer ear. Glue 2 ears behind each rabbit head on the back of each finger. For the tails, glue ½″ white pom-poms to the backs of fingers.

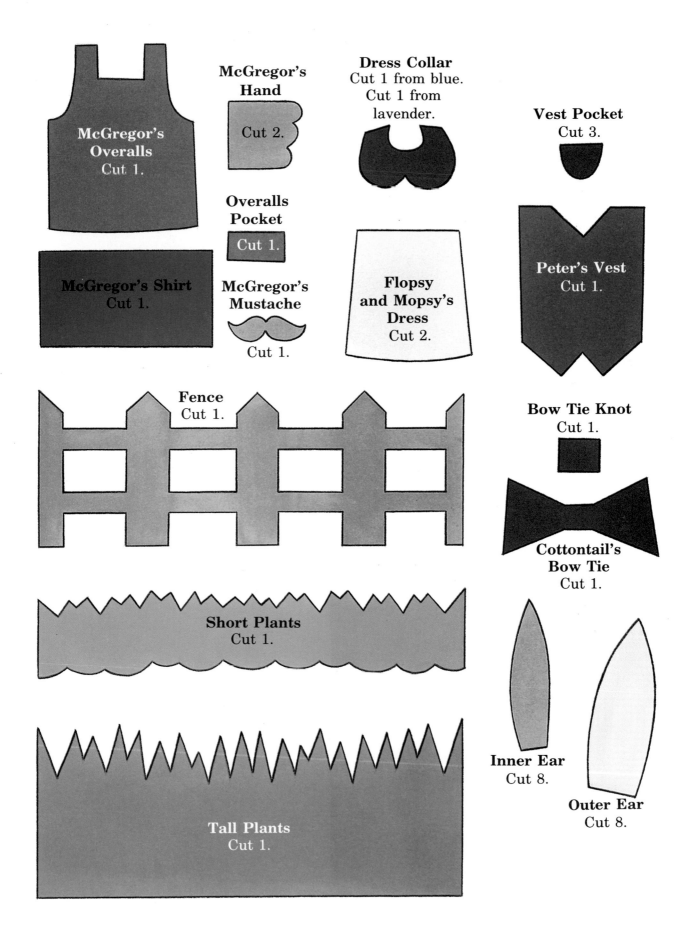

McGregor's Overalls
Cut 1.

McGregor's Hand
Cut 2.

Dress Collar
Cut 1 from blue.
Cut 1 from lavender.

Vest Pocket
Cut 3.

Overalls Pocket
Cut 1.

McGregor's Shirt
Cut 1.

McGregor's Mustache
Cut 1.

Flopsy and Mopsy's Dress
Cut 2.

Peter's Vest
Cut 1.

Fence
Cut 1.

Bow Tie Knot
Cut 1.

Cottontail's Bow Tie
Cut 1.

Short Plants
Cut 1.

Inner Ear
Cut 8.

Outer Ear
Cut 8.

Tall Plants
Cut 1.

127

Buddy Bear's Friends

Everybody needs a beary special friend to cuddle, to talk to, or to share cocoa and cookies with. Buddy Bear's friends are simple to make and certain to be hugs of fun!

You will need (for 1 bear):
Tracing paper
1 yard (54"-wide) sheared-fur fabric
¼ yard of plaid flannel fabric
Thread to match fabrics
Polyester stuffing
Embroidery needle
Scrap of black felt
2 (½") black shank buttons
2 (2") pieces of black yarn

Note: When working with fur, trim the pile from the seam allowance as close to the fabric as possible before stitching the seam. If necessary after stitching, fluff the fur near the seams to keep them as invisible as possible.

1. Enlarge the patterns as indicated. Transfer the patterns and markings to the tracing paper. Add ¼" seam allowances to gridded patterns only. (The patterns not on the grid already include ¼" seam allowances.) Cut out the patterns. Pin the pattern pieces to the fabric and cut them out as indicated.

2. Turn under the raw edges of the inner ears ¼". Referring to the pattern for placement, slipstitch 1 inner ear to the right side of 1 ear. Repeat for other ear.

3. With right sides facing and raw edges aligned, stitch 1 ear front and 1 ear back together, leaving the straight edges open. Clip the curves and turn. Repeat for the other ear. Baste the pleats in the ears where indicated on the pattern.

4. With raw edges aligned and pleat at the top of the head, pin 1 ear, plaid side down, to the right side of each body front where indicated. Baste in place.

5. With right sides facing and raw edges aligned, stitch the 2 body front pieces together along the center front seam. Stitch darts on each body back. Then stitch the 2 body back pieces together along the center back seam.

6. With right sides facing and raw edges aligned, stitch the bear front and back together around the sides, arms, and head, leaving the bottom edge open where indicated for placement of the legs. Clip the curves and turn.

7. With right sides facing and raw edges aligned, stitch 2 leg sections together, leaving the straight edge open. Repeat for the other leg. Clip the curves and turn. Align the center front and center back seams and stuff each leg firmly. Baste the tops of the legs closed.

8. With raw edges aligned and feet pointing toward the head, pin the front of the legs to the bottom of the body front only. (Keep the body back free.) Stitch the legs in place.

9. Stuff the bear's head, neck, arms, and body firmly. Stuff the area where the arms meet the body lightly to allow the arms to bend.

10. Turn under the raw edge of the body back opening ¼" and slipstitch it in place over the raw edges of the legs.

11. Turn under the raw edges of the paw pads ¼". Center a pad on the bottom of each foot and slipstitch it in place.

12. Referring to the pattern for placement, sew on button eyes. Slipstitch the felt nose in place. To make the mouth, tack the yarn in place with black thread (see photo).

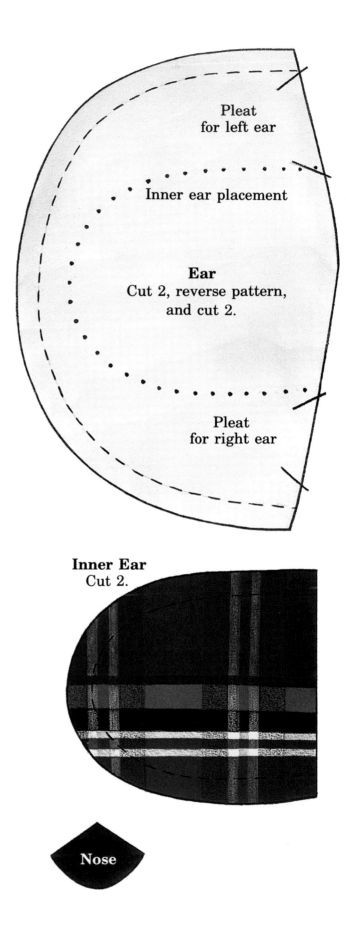

Pleat for left ear

Inner ear placement

Ear
Cut 2, reverse pattern, and cut 2.

Pleat for right ear

Inner Ear
Cut 2.

Nose

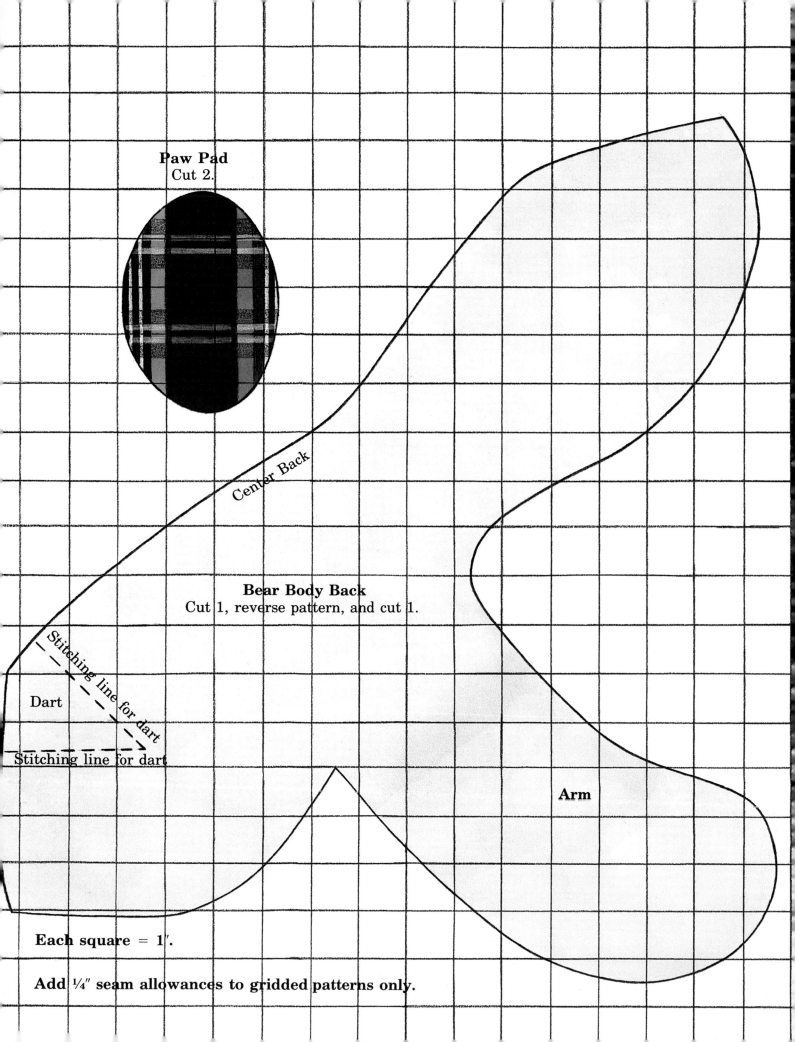

Paw Pad
Cut 2.

Center Back

Bear Body Back
Cut 1, reverse pattern, and cut 1.

Stitching line for dart

Dart

Stitching line for dart

Arm

Each square = 1″.

Add ¼″ seam allowances to gridded patterns only.

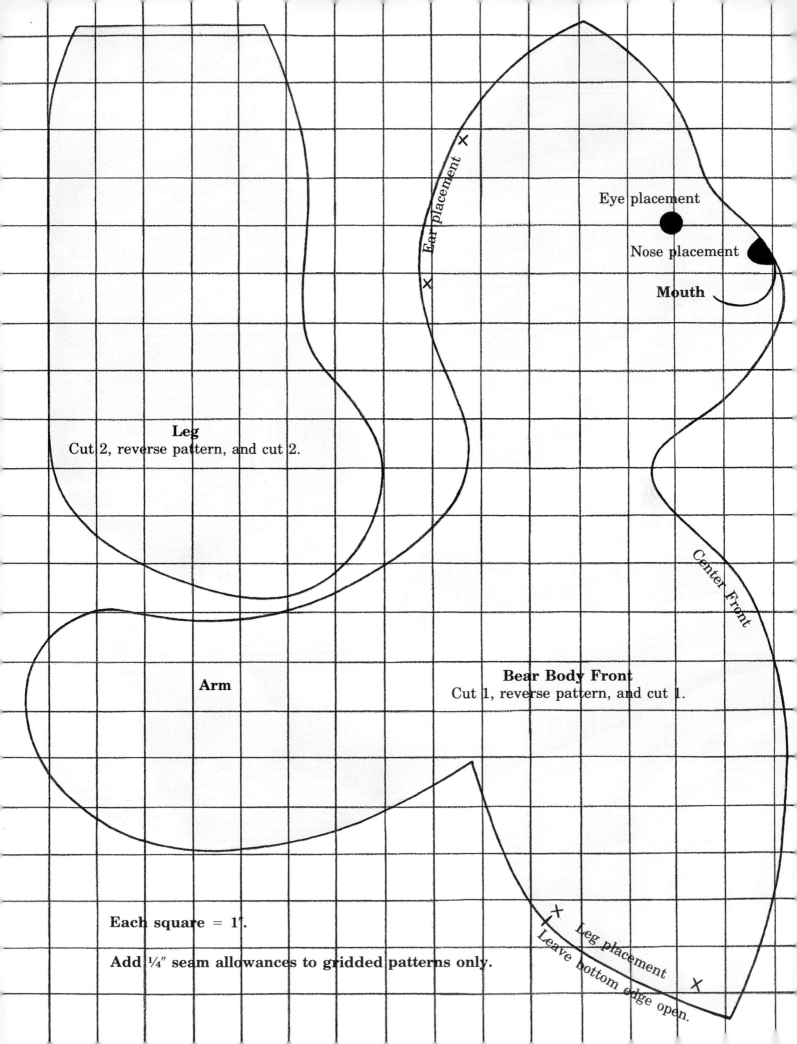

Leg
Cut 2, reverse pattern, and cut 2.

Ear placement

Eye placement

Nose placement

Mouth

Center Front

Arm

Bear Body Front
Cut 1, reverse pattern, and cut 1.

Leg placement

Leave bottom edge open.

Each square = 1".

Add ¼" seam allowances to gridded patterns only.

Paw Puppet

A perfect fit for little paws, this puppet will entertain Buddy Bear's friends and your friends, too.

You will need:
Tracing paper
½ yard of sheared-fur fabric
Scrap of plaid flannel fabric
Scrap of black felt
Thread to match
2 (⁷⁄₁₆″) round black shank buttons
2 (2″) pieces of black yarn
Embroidery needle
2 (6″) squares of lightweight white cotton
    fabric
Polyester stuffing

Note: When working with fur, trim the pile from the seam allowance as close to the fabric as possible before stitching the seam. If necessary, fluff the fur near the seams with the point of a needle after stitching, to keep seams as invisible as possible.

1. Trace and transfer the patterns. Cut out. Pin the pattern pieces to the fabric and cut out as indicated.

2. With right sides facing and raw edges aligned, stitch the head pieces together around the front between A and B. Clip the curves.

3. With right sides facing and raw edges aligned, match the Xs on the head front to the Xs on the body front. Stitch the head and body together between the Xs.

4. Referring to the pattern for placement, sew on the button eyes. Slipstitch the felt nose in place. To make the mouth, tack the yarn in place with black thread. (See photo.)

5. Turn under ⅛″ on the raw edges of the inner ear pieces. Referring to the pattern for placement, slipstitch 1 inner ear to 1 ear front. Repeat for the other ear.

6. With right sides facing and raw edges aligned, pin the front of the bear to the back at the sides and around the head. Stitch together, leaving the bottom straight edge open. Clip the curves. Turn up a ¼″ hem around the bottom opening and slipstitch in place. Turn right side out.

Add ¼″ seam allowances to patterns.

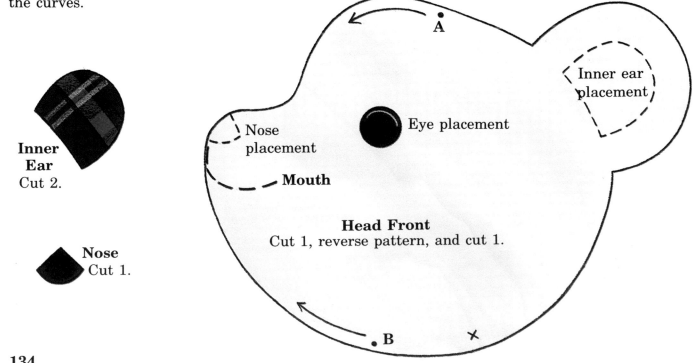

Inner Ear
Cut 2.

Nose
Cut 1.

Nose placement

Eye placement

Inner ear placement

Mouth

A

B

Head Front
Cut 1, reverse pattern, and cut 1.

7. With right sides facing and raw edges aligned, stitch the 2 (6″) white cotton squares together, leaving an opening for turning. Trim corners and turn. Stuff loosely with polyester stuffing. Slipstitch the opening closed.

8. Insert this stuffed bag into the head of the puppet. No tacking is necessary. The bag can be removed when a child plays with the puppet or left in place to give the head added support when Buddy Bear uses it.

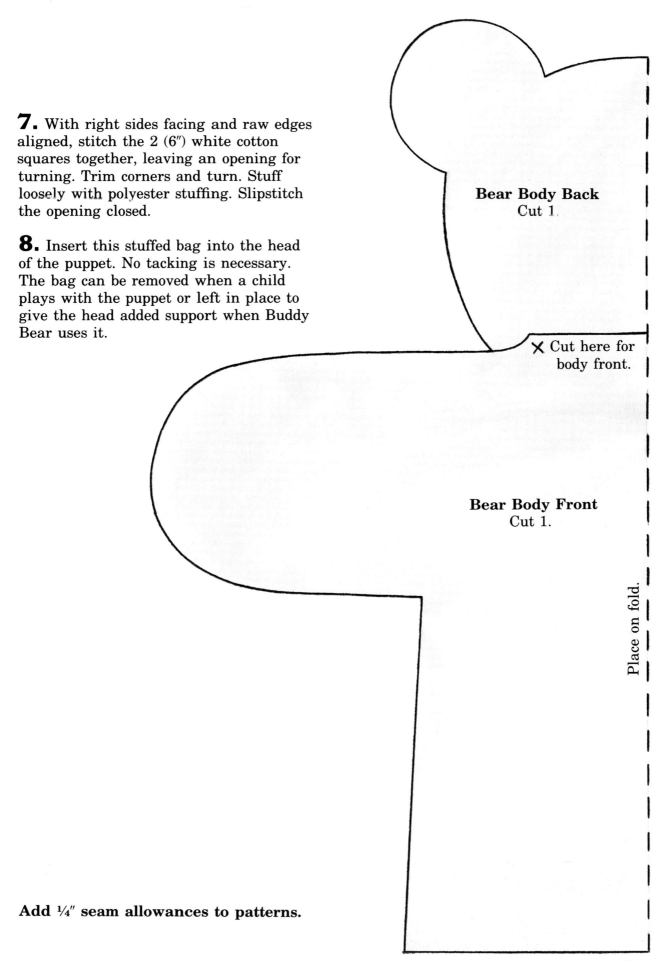

Bear Body Back
Cut 1.

✕ Cut here for body front.

Bear Body Front
Cut 1.

Place on fold.

Add ¼″ seam allowances to patterns.

Boo-boo Birdies

When the little hurts seem like big boo-boos, it's Boo-boo Birdie to the rescue. Place ice in a plastic bag, put the bag inside the bird, and close the fastener. Apply Boo-boo and tender loving care, and little tots will be assured of a quick recovery.

You will need (for 1 bird):
Tracing paper
½ yard of terry cloth
Thread to match
⅛ yard of washable contrasting fabric
4″ (½″-wide) Velcro
Crewel needle
1 yard of black yarn
32″ (1″-wide) ribbon
Small zip-top plastic bag for ice

1. Trace and transfer the patterns for the wings, beak, and legs. Cut out.

2. For the body, cut a 9″ square from the terry cloth. Round off all 4 corners of the square. Then cut out the wings.

3. Cut out the legs and beak from the contrasting fabric.

4. Zigzag-stitch around the edges of the wings and the body to prevent raveling.

5. Fold the beak on the fold line, with right sides facing. Stitch the short edge of the triangle closed, using a ¼″ seam. Trim the point and turn right side out. Press. Place the unstitched edge of the beak on 1 edge of the 9″ square, ¾″ from 1 corner. (Figure A.) Baste in place.

6. Fold the square in half diagonally, from the corner nearest the beak to the opposite corner. (The corner nearest the beak will be the head.) Pin the center of the wings to the fold line about 3″ below the top of the head. Unfold the square and zigzag-stitch the wings along the fold line.

7. With right sides facing, sew the leg pieces together, leaving a 2½″ opening in the center of 1 long edge. Trim the corners, clip the curves, and turn right side out. Press. Slipstitch the opening closed. Fold the legs in half and slide them apart slightly. (Figure A.) Baste the fold of the

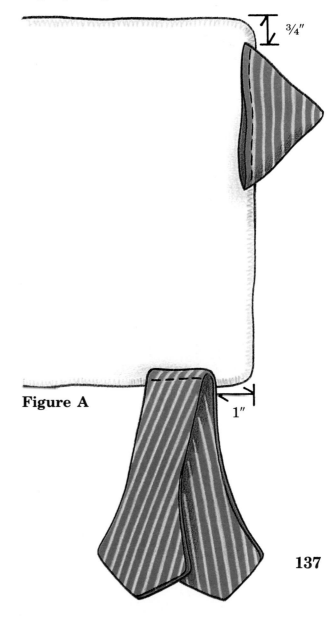

Figure A

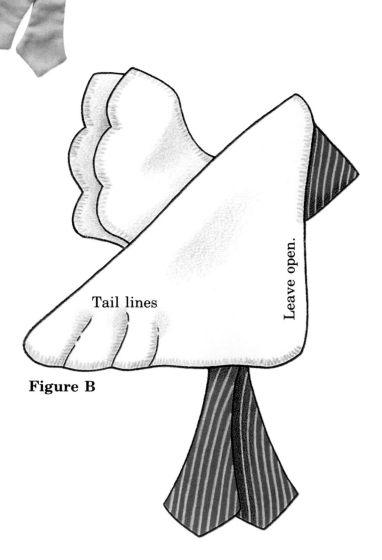

legs to the square, about 1″ from corner below the beak.

8. Refold the square into a triangle. Zigzag-stitch the edges together from the top of head to the bottom of the beak. Leave the area under the beak unstitched as far as the corner.

9. Sew the hook side of the Velcro strip to 1 side of the opening below the beak and the fuzz side to the other side of the opening. Close the Velcro opening. Beginning at the end of the Velcro, stitch the entire bottom edge closed.

10. Zigzag-stitch the tail lines as shown. (Figure B.)

11. For the eyes, make a French knot with the yarn on each side of the head. (See photo.)

12. Cut the ribbon into 2 (16″) lengths. Tie a bow with 1 length. Then tie a bow around the first bow with the second length. Tack the bow just under the beak.

Tail lines

Leave open.

Figure B

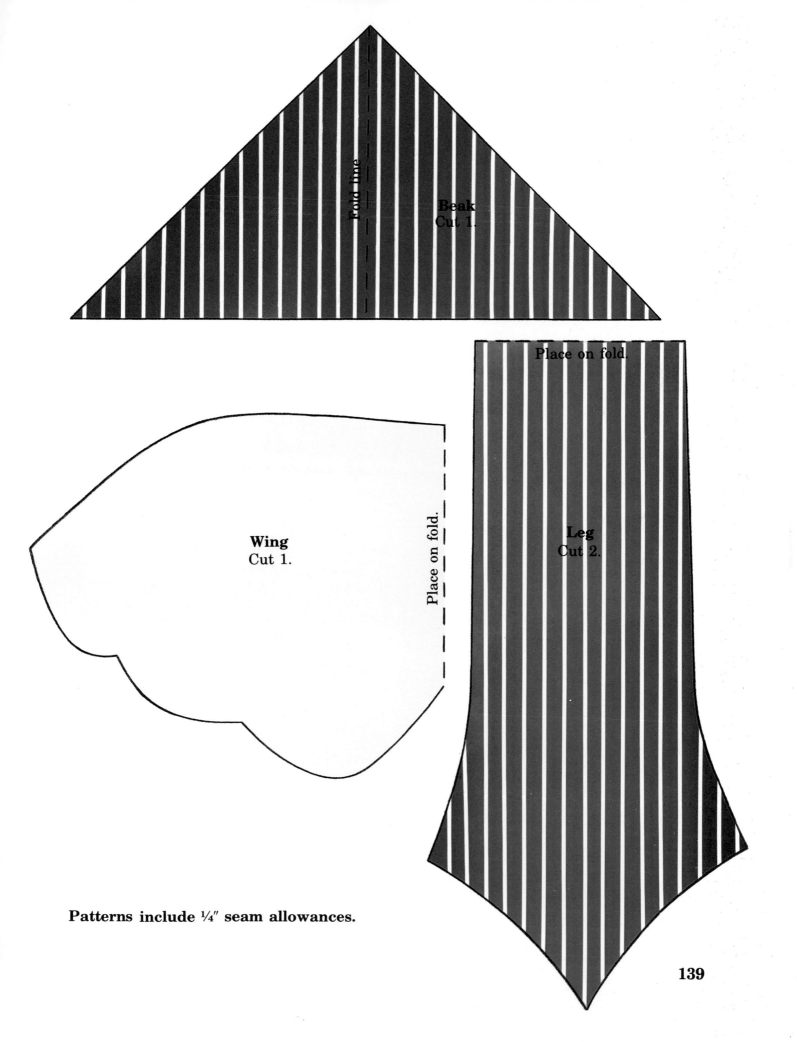

Beak
Cut 1.

Fold line

Place on fold.

Wing
Cut 1.

Place on fold.

Leg
Cut 2.

Patterns include ¼″ seam allowances.

139

Happy Trails

Ride 'em, cowboy! While searching for lost cattle, wild stallions, and Black Bart, your wrangler and his trusty pony are sure to ride down lots of happy trails.

You will need:
Tracing paper and carbon paper
¼ sheet of ¾" cabinet-grade plywood
¼ sheet of ¼" cabinet-grade plywood
Electric jigsaw or coping saw
Wood rasp (file)
Sandpaper
Wood glue
Wood clamps
Electric drill and ½" drill bit
Vise
38" (½") wooden dowel
Varnish
Paintbrush
Heavy white yarn
Staple gun and ½" staples
Hammer
Chamois scraps
4 feet (½"-wide) leather belting or
    decorative cording
Awl
Leather rivets

1. Trace the patterns and cut them out. Using carbon paper, transfer the head and eyebrow patterns to the good side of the ¾″ plywood and the cheek and face patterns to the good side of the ¼″ plywood. Using the electric jigsaw or coping saw, cut out each piece as marked.

2. Using the wood rasp, file and round all of the cut edges. Then sand each piece.

3. Glue 1 cheek to 1 face as indicated on the pattern. Clamp together until the glue dries. Glue the remaining cheek and face together. (To save sanding later, always clean up excess glue with a damp rag before it dries.) Clamp and let dry.

4. Before drilling, clamp the head, with the bottom up, to a tabletop or in a vise. Drill a 1″-deep hole in the base of the head where indicated on the pattern.

5. When the cheek/face units are dry, glue them to opposite sides of the head, where indicated on the pattern. Clamp and let dry.

6. For the eyes, cut 2 (¾″) pieces from 1 end of the dowel. Round 1 end of each eye piece with the rasp and sand. Glue 1 eye, flat end down, and 1 eyebrow to the head, referring to the pattern for placement. Glue the remaining eye and eyebrow to the other side of the head. Clamp and let dry. When dry, sand all surfaces.

7. Glue the remaining length of dowel in the hole in the base of the head. Let dry. Clamp the dowel in a vise and apply 1 coat of varnish to the head. When dry, apply a second coat of varnish. Let the varnish dry.

8. Cut the yarn into 10″ lengths. (The number of lengths needed will depend on

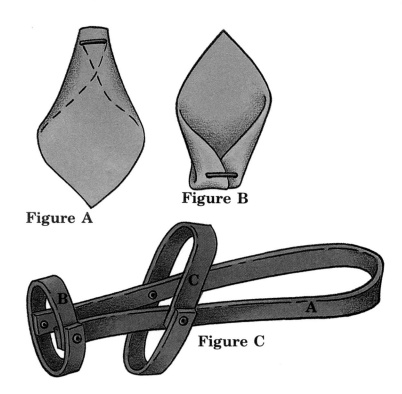

Figure A

Figure B

Figure C

the thickness of the yarn used.) Staple the center of the yarn pieces in place down the center of the back of the head, with the staples parallel to the sides of the head. Firmly hammer the staples into the wood. Then knot the strands of yarn together to cover the staples.

9. Cut 2 ears from the chamois. Fold the sides of 1 ear toward the center. With the folded side down and the point toward the bottom of the head, staple the ear to the head where indicated. (Figure A.) Hammer the staple into the wood. Lift the ear and staple it again. (Figure B.) Again, hammer the staple into the wood. Repeat for the other ear.

10. To make the bridle, cut the leather belting into 3 strips: A–28″; B–6½″; C–12½″. Wrap strip B around the muzzle and mark where the ends overlap. Using the awl, punch holes in both ends of the strip at this point. (Figure C.) Punch a hole in the end of strip A. Rivet 1 end of strip A with both ends of strip B on top of it. Punch a hole in the opposite end of strip A and the opposite side of strip B. Rivet them together. Slip the bridle over the muzzle of the horse again. Then wrap strip C over the head (see photo) and mark the hole placement as you did for strip B. Rivet strip C to strip A on both sides of head. (A bridle may also be made by tying pieces of cord together.)

11. Cut off the bottom of the dowel to the proper height for the child. Round and sand the end smooth.

Ear
Cut 2.

Face
Cut 1 from ¼″ plywood, reverse pattern, and cut 1.

Placement line
for cheek

Drill here.

Match dots and continue pattern across page.

End mane here.

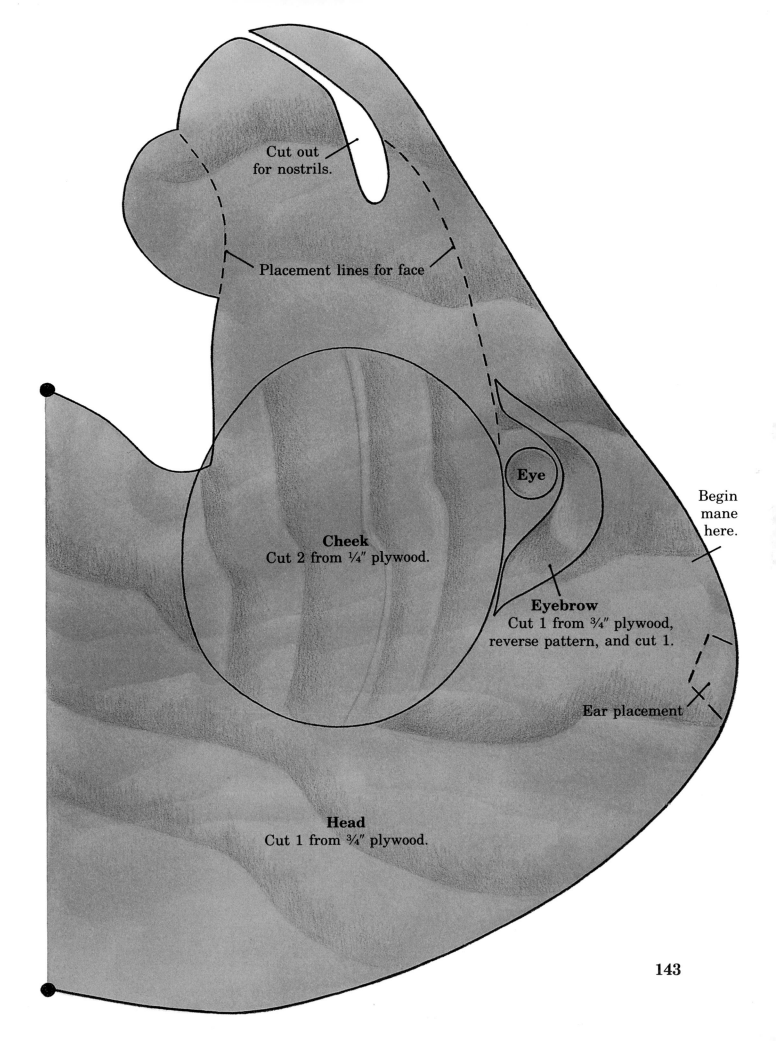

Cut out
for nostrils.

Placement lines for face

Eye

Begin
mane
here.

Cheek
Cut 2 from ¼″ plywood.

Eyebrow
Cut 1 from ¾″ plywood,
reverse pattern, and cut 1.

Ear placement

Head
Cut 1 from ¾″ plywood.

143

Designers & Contributors

Barbara Ball, Flying Angels, 12; Poppers Popping, 27; Glitter Tree, 55; Foldout Cards, 58.

Micheal Baltzell, Happy Trails, 140.

Melanie Barrentine Barnes, Holiday Pins, 89.

Amy Albert Bloom, Parachute Santa, 70; SS Teddy Towel, 106.

Kendall Boggs, Christmas Collars, 99.

Shirley Burgess, Letter-Gator, 82.

Susan Z. Douglas, Snowflakes, 52.

Sandra Lounsberry Foose, Paper Heart Cluster, 64.

Connie Formby, Invitations, 8; Ho-Ho Hats, 11; Dancing Shoes, 15; Santas Sitting, 30.

Dot Formby, Golden Stars, 17; Stockings for Stuffing, 24.

Deborah Hastings, Storybook Headboards, 116; Rock-a-bye Baby, 122.

Linda Hendrickson, Porcupine Pincushion, 76; Sock Hop Slippers, 96; Cross-stitched Longjohns, 110; Boo-boo Birdies, 136.

Mary-Gray Hunter, Herb Garden, 78.

Janet Mysse, Muffler, Mittens, and Cap, 113.

Steve Schutt, Paw Puppet, 133.

Betsy Scott, Spray-Painted Tees, 80; Stamp It Out, 86; Self-Portrait, 92; Frog Santa Sweatshirt, 103.

Elizabeth Taliaferro, Treats for Tasting, 34; Shakes for Sipping, 38.

Carol M. Tipton, Garden Glove Puppet, 125; Buddy Bear's Friends, 128.

Elizabeth Valsecchi, Cork Reindeer, 66.

Madeline O'Brien White, Kazoos for Playing, 22; Angel Gift Bags, 44; Marbleized Paper, 46; Felt Faces, 48; A Frame-Up, 72.

Special thanks to the following shops in Birmingham, Alabama for sharing their resources: **Applause Dancewear & Accessories; Chocolate Soup, Inc.; Huffstutler's Hardware Home Center; Jack N' Jill Shop; Sikes Children's Shoes; Smith's Variety of Mountain Brook; Vestavia Hills Apothecary.**